THE BRONTËS IN BRUSSELS

By the same author

Down the Belliard Steps: Discovering the Brontës in Brussels

THE BRONTËS IN BRUSSELS

Helen MacEwan

PETER OWEN PUBLISHERS
London and Chicago

PETER OWEN PUBLISHERS
81 Ridge Road, London N8 9NP

Peter Owen books are distributed in the USA and Canada by
Independent Publishers Group/Trafalgar Square
814 North Franklin Street, Chicago, IL 60610, USA

First published in Great Britain 2014 by Peter Owen Publishers

ISBN 978-0-7206-1588-3

A catalogue record for this book is available
from the British Library

Printed and bound by CPI Group (UK) Ltd, Croydon, CR0 4YY

CONTENTS

ACKNOWLEDGEMENTS

My fascination with the stay of Charlotte and Emily Brontë in Brussels has developed over years of organizing guided walks and talks on Brontë-related subjects in the Belgian capital since setting up the Brussels Brontë Group in 2006. This has brought me into contact with enthusiasts and scholars who have added to my knowledge of the history of Brussels – a beautiful city in the Brontës' time and one that retains much charm despite the destruction wrought by urban developers. Although many of the old streets Charlotte and Emily wandered along have vanished, there is still plenty to remind us of the Brussels of their time, as I hope this book shows.

I have been assisted by friendly historians, librarians, archivists, city guides, researchers both professional and amateur. I am indebted to Eric Ruijssenaars, whose books *Charlotte Brontë's Promised Land: The Pensionnat Heger and Other Brontë Places in Brussels* and *The Pensionnat Revisited: More Light Shed on the Brussels of the Brontës* first launched me on a voyage of discovery of the sisters' time in the city. I would also like to thank Brian Bracken, indefatigable Brontës-in-Brussels researcher, for answering numerous queries and for reading my manuscript and making suggestions; Paul Gretton and Patsy Stoneman for also reading the book and making comments; Selina Busch for her skill and patience in drawing the maps; Sam for helping me with his encyclopaedic knowledge of the streets of nineteenth-century Brussels and with technical aspects of the illustrations; Margaret Smith, editor of Charlotte Brontë's letters, for giving her blessing for the use of her translation of Charlotte's letters to Constantin Heger; Sue Lonoff for allowing me to reproduce her translations of some of Charlotte's and Emily's French essays (*devoirs*); François Fierens, the great-great-great-grandson of Constantin Heger, for letting me use images of some of the *devoirs* in his possession; Roel Jacobs, history consultant to VisitBrussels, the tourist board, for answering queries; the staff of the Brussels Archives and the Royal Library of Belgium for their help with my requests for images in their collections; and Sarah Laycock at the Brontë Parsonage Museum for her help with images owned by the Brontë Society. And, finally, my husband José Miguel for all his support.

Helen MacEwan
Brussels, 2014

FOREWORD

Genius is not enough. It has to find the right place to develop, and for Charlotte Brontë that place was Brussels. As Helen MacEwan says, the two years she spent there 'changed her for ever'. She and her sister, Emily, went to Brussels in their early to mid-twenties in order to acquire sufficient French, also some German and, in Emily's case, music in preparation for a school they hoped to open at home in Haworth Parsonage, West Yorkshire. But Brussels was also Charlotte's 'promised land', a place of exquisite pictures and venerable cathedrals. As she told her friend Ellen Nussey, she had an 'urgent thirst' for more than formal accomplishments, 'to see – to know – to learn'. Brushing aside a teaching opportunity, she stated in a letter dated 7 August 1841 that she felt 'such a vehement impatience of restraint and steady work; such a strong wish for wings ... I was tantalized with the consciousness of faculties unexercised'.

This illustrated guide introduces us to the Brussels that the Brontë sisters encountered in 1842–3. It lays out vital information about this foreign venture in the Brontës' somewhat constricted lives as young women of small means and big dreams. Helen MacEwan, who lives in the city, started up a literary society, the Brussels Brontë Group, and her previous book, *Down the Belliard Steps: Discovering the Brontës in Brussels*, is about the inception of the society, its members and walks in the footsteps of the gifted sisters. Now she gives us a biographical close-up of the Brontës on the ground in Brussels, starting with a vivid scene of their arrival in the city and their reception at the school of their choice, the Pensionnat Heger. We discover the history of the area around the school, whom the sisters knew and whom they did not care to know, what they thought of the Belgians, how Emily dressed and how they felt as foreigners and Protestants in a Catholic environment.

Part of the pleasure of this admirably clear and readable book is the detail of the sisters' lives on an ordinary day. We find out what they ate – the *pistolets* for breakfast; the sauces; the pears from the school's garden stewed in white wine – in contrast to meals at the Parsonage; where they sat in the classroom; where they slept upstairs in the long dormitory and what their sleeping arrangements can tell us about their relation to the other boarders; and why the demoiselles were not permitted to walk along a certain garden path the Brontës frequented. We see the two walking together: Emily, who was taller and unable to adjust, leaning on her readier elder sister. There is a charming picture of the walled garden with its *berceaux*, arbours covered with vines, as a place for exercise in the heart of the city. As Helen MacEwan explains with well-chosen quotes from fiction, this garden also 'fired Charlotte's imagination'.

The Rue d'Isabelle, the sunken road where the Brontës lived, is now no more, but the book restores what is lost, describing the site and layout of the school at the bottom of the Belliard steps in relation to buildings in present-day Brussels and in relation, too, to places of worship, which survive much as they were in the Brontës' time. Maps and abundant illustrations show exactly where the sisters went: the park, the fashionable streets in the upper city, the back alleys of the lower city, the outskirts. This Brussels swims into sight as never before. Here is a contemporary painting of women lining up for confession in the Cathedral, where in the summer of 1843 Charlotte is driven to make a confession. Guided by this book, visitors to Brussels will be able to find their own way into this storied past.

How did the Brontës develop as writers during these years just before the great flowering of their gifts in the poems and novels that would bring them universal fame? A letter from Charlotte in July 1842 records Emily's rapid progress in French, German, music and drawing. At the Pensionnat the promise of

The *grand berceau* (arbour) in the Pensionnat garden
Brontë Parsonage Museum

these two obscure young women is seen for the first time. Their
gifts are honed and exercised by a born teacher, M. Heger, who
trains Charlotte how to rein and release passion with that tension
between abandon and decorum that characterizes her writer's voice.
A new precision compels Charlotte to break with the high-life
fantasies of her prolonged juvenilia. Almost before she knows it
Charlotte is in love with her exacting 'Master', a love bound up with
the play of language, the interplay of the French he confers on her
and the English she offers to him, fuelled by her rising ambition.

During Charlotte's second year, when she remains on her
own at the school, her love of this married man becomes obsessive.
Helen MacEwan's grasp of this situation, fraught with Charlotte's
envy of the well-groomed and good-looking Mme Heger, directress
of the Pensionnat, is both dramatic and balanced in showing how
differently Madame appears to others.

And all the time a quantum leap is taking place in Charlotte's
increasingly impressive *devoirs*. These dare to open up a dialogue
with her teacher. Emily dared more: she is openly rebellious,
preferring originality to the discipline M. Heger requires. His

standards of terseness and correctness, and the sisters' remarkable progress in French are evident in this book's selections from their Brussels essays.

What more did Charlotte want? Her *Letter from a Poor Painter* reveals this to her teacher with astonishing candour. Here, with the thinnest of fictional veils, is her understanding of her own latent 'genius', demanding the fuller recognition that will bring it on. She craves her Master's words quite as much as she longs, as a woman, for his response. A susceptible man, working on rare gifts of feeling and eloquence, which he has the calibre to estimate at their true value, he finds it necessary in the end to withdraw from the obsession he has aroused.

There follow Charlotte's alternately passionate and painfully tight-lipped letters to M. Heger after her return to Haworth. These four letters are included here in full. The love was to find extraordinary expression in the new kinds of heroes – keen to discern the hidden nature of women worth knowing – in Charlotte's two 'Brussels novels', most obviously in the irascible teacher, M. Paul, in her later masterpiece, *Villette*. Telling extracts from *Villette*, the novel suffused with its author's Brussels experience, are also included in this volume, which covers every aspect of this journey abroad for two untried women of genius in the making.

Lyndall Gordon
Author of Charlotte Brontë: A Passionate Life

AUTHOR'S NOTE

This is intended to be a concise guide to Charlotte's and Emily Brontë's stay in Brussels in 1842–3, providing the biographical facts we have about their time there and information on the Brussels they knew, the city Charlotte depicted in her first novel *The Professor* (written in 1845–6 and published posthumously) and her fourth and last, *Villette* (published in 1853). In the earlier book Brussels is named, as are its actual streets. In the later, more personal novel, into which Charlotte put much more of her emotional experience while in Belgium, she sought concealment. Brussels becomes 'Villette', and its streets and monuments are disguised under fictional names, or else names of real places are deliberately mixed up.

Both of them draw heavily on Charlotte's life in Belgium. Of course we should not forget that they are works of fiction; Lucy Snowe's M. Paul in *Villette* is not an exact portrait of Charlotte's teacher Constantin Heger, and Mme Beck's Pensionnat in *Villette* or Mlle Reuter's in *The Professor* are not in every respect the Pensionnat Heger, the boarding-school where the Brontë sisters stayed. But although Charlotte changed and invented whenever necessary for her creative ends, she was often startlingly literal in her use of people and places she knew. Many of her Yorkshire acquaintances recognized themselves in the pages of *Shirley* (1849), into which, for example, not content with portraying her old school friend Mary Taylor as Rose Yorke, she also transplanted Mary's entire family as the Yorke family, down to such details as the death of Mary Taylor's sister Martha while in Brussels (Rose's younger sister Jessy dies abroad). She also described features of the Taylors' house. Similarly, in *Villette* she made liberal use of numerous aspects of the Pensionnat and its inmates and of many other places in Brussels that are recognizable from her descriptions.

I hope that this brief guide will provide a glimpse of the real experiences and the real city on which Charlotte drew in *The Professor* and *Villette*. If you are not familiar with these novels you might like to turn first to the plot summaries near the end of this book. For total immersion in the Brontës' Brussels world, once you have finished this guide read *Villette* and *The Professor*, above all *Villette*, the haunting and deeply personal novel of Charlotte Brontë's maturity.

Charlotte Brontë waving goodbye across the Channel. In this cartoon of herself in a letter to her best friend Ellen Nussey, dated 6 March 1843, Charlotte, always dissatisfied with her own appearance, portrays herself as stunted with a head too large for her body. In contrast, Ellen, who is being courted by an admirer, could be the graceful heroine of a Victorian novel.
Brontë Parsonage Museum

Rue Royale and the Park, with the Cathedral in the background. The mansion on the left-hand side is the Hôtel Errera, with the entrance to the Belliard steps just beyond it.

E.M. Wimperis, illustration for The Professor, *Smith, Elder and Co., London, 1873*

Belgium! I repeat the word, now as I sit alone near midnight. It stirs my world of the past like a summons to resurrection; the graves unclose, the dead are raised; thoughts, feelings, memories that slept, are seen by me ascending from the clods . . .

This is Belgium, reader. Look! don't call the picture a flat or a dull one – it was neither flat nor dull to me when I first beheld it. When I left Ostend on a mild February morning, and found myself on the road to Brussels, nothing could look vapid to me.

– *The Professor*, Chapter 7

I

TWO NEW ARRIVALS AT THE PENSIONNAT DE DEMOISELLES

On the morning of Tuesday 15 February 1842 three visitors from England could be seen walking down Brussels' Rue Royale, as elegant carriages rattled by, past the park, to and from Place Royale. From their appearance it was clear that these visitors were not members of the carriage-owning class themselves. They had the weary look of people who had arrived late the previous night after a day in an uncomfortable public stagecoach following the fourteen-hour Channel crossing to Ostend. They had the half-dazed, half-excited look of people on their first continental trip.

It was a dull grey day. It would soon be spring, and the park would be alive with music and crowds, but that morning its avenues were almost deserted, the branches of the trees bare against an overcast sky.

The visitors were a tall white-haired clergyman and his two daughters, young women in their twenties. The younger and taller sister had a dreamy look, as if she found her own thoughts as interesting as the sights of this strange city. Her old-fashioned and somewhat dishevelled clothes suggested that, although she was the more attractive of the two girls, dress did not rank very high in her priorities. The elder, smaller and plainer sister had a different way of looking around, as if noticing everything and storing it up for future use. The expression on her face was both excited and apprehensive. She, too, was old-fashioned in appearance but neatly dressed. It seemed as if she did care what impression she made.

Little houses in Rue d'Isabelle
Brussels City Archives

The three were accompanied by another clergyman, an Englishman who, unlike them, appeared to know his way around Brussels. He led them to a little square opposite the park where there was a statue with the name 'General Belliard' on the plinth. It stood at the top of a long, steep and rather dark stairway which plunged down to a quiet street at a much lower level and parallel to Rue Royale. The group paused for a moment at the top of the stairway, gazing down. Both girls now looked apprehensive.

'That', their guide told them, 'is the Rue d'Isabelle.'

He led them down the four flights of steps into the street below.

On leaving their hotel earlier that morning the new arrivals had done a little sightseeing. They had passed through old streets full of character, narrow and winding, with tall irregular gabled houses, before walking through a much newer part of town, Place Royale and its mansions. The tranquil street where they now found themselves did not fall into either category; it was narrow but had neat symmetrical rows of modest houses. Some of the smaller ones were as quaint and charming as cottages or almshouses, more in place in a village than so close to the bustle of the royal quarter. The door they stopped at, however, opposite the foot of the steps, belonged to a larger building with tall windows.

Down here the noise of the carriage wheels far above was muted, and the elegant thoroughfare at the top of the steps seemed to belong to another world. Rue d'Isabelle was a peaceful spot in the heart of the city.

A brass plate on the door announced 'Pensionnat de Demoiselles Heger-Parent'.

Even without this indication, the hum of activity they could hear from within the building would have told them that it was a school. They rang the bell. A few minutes later the father and his two shy, awkward daughters were being presented to the directress of the boarding school by Rev. Jenkins, the clergyman who had guided them and who introduced himself as the British Chaplain in Brussels.

'Mme Heger, this is Mr Brontë, and these are his daughters, Charlotte and Emily.'

FRANCES SAT VERY QUIET, HER ELBOW
ON HER KNEE

Frances Henri at her aunt's grave in the Protestant Cemetery
in Brussels.
Edmund Dulac, illustration for The Professor, *Dent, London, 1922*

2

WHAT BROUGHT THE BRONTËS
TO BRUSSELS?

In February 1842 Charlotte Brontë was twenty-five, Emily Brontë twenty-three. Only four of the Reverend Patrick Brontë's six children had survived childhood: Charlotte, Branwell the only son of the family (then twenty-four), Emily and Anne, who was twenty-two. The two eldest girls, Maria and Elizabeth, had died before reaching their teens. The children's mother, Maria Branwell, had died when Charlotte was only five, and her sister – Aunt Branwell – had come to take care of them at the grey parsonage in Haworth on the Yorkshire moors.

In 1842 the two young women who only a few years later were to write two of the world's best-selling novels, *Jane Eyre* and *Wuthering Heights*, were still unknown. But all four surviving siblings had since childhood been compulsive writers, collaborating in creating wild, romantic stories set in imaginary countries, filling page after tiny page of miniature notebooks with minuscule handwriting almost impossible for outsiders to decipher.

When not 'scribbling', as they themselves called it, they were out roaming the moors. But much as they loved being at home together writing or walking the girls knew they had to earn a living and contribute to the family finances. Papa was a poor clergyman, and the brilliant but erratic Branwell could not be relied on to help support the family. He was never able to hold down a job for long and in later years would run up debts to fund his drinking.

Portrait of the Brontë sisters by Branwell Brontë, *c.* 1834, when he
was seventeen. From left to right: Anne aged fourteen, Emily sixteen
and Charlotte eighteen
National Portrait Gallery

They all dreamed of being published writers, but for the
moment the only paid work open to the girls was teaching, at
schools or as governesses. They had tried it. But they had not
enjoyed the experience, and, with the possible exception of Anne,
their success can be gauged from a remark made by a former employer of Charlotte's: 'I once had the misfortune to employ a
governess of the name of Brontë.'

One reason for their unhappiness as teachers was that they

Branwell Brontë: self-portrait drawn
c. 1840, when he was twenty-three

were homesick whenever separated and away from Haworth.
Charlotte saw a possible solution. They could open their own
boarding-school, either in the Parsonage or elsewhere. She eventually opted for the Parsonage itself, despite the logistical problems
of using a house with just four bedrooms and the drawback of
having a brother who, when at home between jobs, had a tendency
to roll in drunk in the small hours and once set his bed curtains on
fire by knocking over a candle.

While working as a governess in September 1841 Charlotte
wrote home to her aunt about this project and about an idea
suggested to her by the experience of her friends Mary and
Martha Taylor, who were improving their languages at a Brussels
boarding-school.

My friends recommend me . . . to delay commencing the
school for six months longer, and . . . to spend the interven-
ing time in some school on the continent . . . I would not go
to France or to Paris. I would go to Brussels, in Belgium . . .
living is there little more than half as dear as it is in England,
and the facilities for education are equal or superior to any
other place in Europe. In half a year, I could acquire a
thorough familiarity with French. I could improve greatly
in Italian, and even get a dash of German . . . Martha Taylor
is now staying in Brussels, at a first-rate establishment there.
I should not think of going to the Château de Koekelberg,
where she is resident, as the terms are much too high; but
if I wrote to her, she, with the assistance of Mrs Jenkins, the
wife of the British Chaplain, would be able to secure me a
cheap and decent residence and respectable protection . . .

. . . I feel an absolute conviction that, if this advantage
were allowed us, it would be the making of us for life. Papa
will perhaps think it a wild and ambitious scheme; but
who ever rose in the world without ambition? When he
left Ireland to go to Cambridge University, he was as ambitious as I am now. I want us *all* to go on. I know we have
talents, and I want them to be turned to account. I look to
you, aunt, to help us.[1]

She was so set on this plan that she wrote in another letter,
'Brussels is my promised land.'[2]

She had another reason for seeing Brussels as her promised
land. After years confined to schoolrooms doing a job she hated,
she was restless. Her youth was going by, and she had seen nothing of life or the world. She longed to experience the culture of a
European city as Mary and Martha were doing. She felt, in her
own words, 'such an urgent thirst to see – to know – to learn'.[3]
Doubtless she dreamed of romance, too, of a real-life hero to take
the place of the ones that had so far existed only in her imagination – in the books she read and the stories she wrote.

Patrick Brontë in old age. He was sixty-five in 1842,
the year Charlotte and Emily went to Brussels.
Brontë Parsonage Museum

From the start she planned to take Emily with her. This
may seem an odd choice since Emily was always the most homesick of the sisters when away from the Parsonage. But she was
Charlotte's favourite sister, and Anne at that time was settled in a
post as a governess.

When Charlotte set her heart on something she had a way of
getting what she wanted. Aunt Branwell was persuaded to fund the
venture, and a suitable school in Brussels was located by the wife
of Evan Jenkins, the British Chaplain, who was the brother of a
friend of Patrick's. Mrs Jenkins recommended Madame Heger's
Pensionnat de demoiselles ('boarding-school for young ladies').
It was agreed that Charlotte and Emily would board there, attend
classes with the other pupils and have special tuition in French.

On 8 February 1842 the two girls and their father set off by train from Leeds in the company of Charlotte's friend Mary Taylor, who was returning to the Château de Koekelberg finishing-school in Brussels, and Mary's brother Joe. Like Lucy Snowe, the heroine of *Villette*, the novel in which Charlotte faithfully recorded much of her Belgian adventure, they did some sightseeing in London before crossing the Channel on the Ostend packet (steam-ship) from London Bridge wharf. After spending a couple of nights at Ostend, on Monday 14 February the party took the *diligence* (stagecoach) to Brussels. On arrival Patrick and Joe Taylor went to the town hall in Grand Place to have their names entered in the police register of foreign visitors; the register can still be seen in the city archives today. The group stayed in the Hôtel de Hollande in Rue de la Putterie, not far from where the Gare Centrale is today. The next morning Mary Taylor, accompanied by her brother, went off to her boarding-school in Koekelberg while the Rev. Jenkins took charge of the Brontës.

Having left his daughters in the care of Madame Heger Patrick spent some days with Rev. Jenkins and his wife seeing the sights of Brussels, also fitting in a visit to the battlefield of Waterloo before returning to Haworth and the Yorkshire moors.

Monuments at the Waterloo battlefield as depicted by H. Gérard, 1842
Royal Library of Belgium

3

THE SITE OF THE PENSIONNAT HEGER TODAY

If you leave the Metro at Parc station and walk down Rue Royale towards Place Royale you will soon see a statue on your right, at the top of a flight of steps leading down to Rue Baron Horta. The statue is of General Augustin Daniel Belliard, a French diplomat who, as France's ambassador in Brussels, assisted the Belgians in negotiating their independence after the 1830 revolution against Dutch rule. In January 1832, coming away from a meeting at the palace, he died of a stroke close to the spot where his statue now stands. His mission had been accomplished; after a shaky start the brand-new country was established on a firm footing.

Belliard's statue was already in place when the Brontës arrived in Brussels, but the steps we see today are not the ones they descended to the Pensionnat, which were steeper and narrower. There were more of them, too, since the school was at a lower level than the site is today.

When you reach the bottom of the steps there is no Pensionnat opposite. It has vanished along with its street, Rue d'Isabelle, which ran parallel to the higher Rue Royale. Today you find yourself in Rue Baron Horta, which is at a right-angle to Rue Royale, running in the same direction as the steps.

At first glance there is nothing at all to indicate that this is the site of the school. To the right is a BNP Paribas Fortis Bank building, to the left the Palais des Beaux-Arts arts centre ('Bozar'), an Art Deco building designed by the architect after whom the street is named, Victor Horta. Bozar is an important place in

26. BRUXELLES — Monument Belliard

The Belliard statue; postcard, *c.* 1900
Brussels City Archives

The Belliard steps; postcard, *c.* 1900
Royal Institute for Cultural Heritage, Brussels; © *KIK–IRPA, Bruxelles*

The Belliard steps today

Brussels, housing the city's main concert hall. Ahead of you is the entrance to a shopping arcade, Galerie Ravenstein.

There is no sign of the Pensionnat, then, and apparently no mention of the Brontës. But walk almost to the end of the street. Before you reach the main entrance of Bozar on the corner with Rue Ravenstein look up and you will see a plaque above a tiny narrow window, placed so high it is rarely spotted by passers-by. It reads:

> Near this site formerly stood the Pensionnat Heger where the writers Charlotte and Emily Brontë studied in 1842–43. This commemorative plaque was placed here by the Brontë Society with the kind permission of the Palais des Beaux-Arts/Paleis voor Schone Kunsten 28–9–79.

The school stood on the site occupied today by Rue Baron Horta and the bank building. It had a large garden which was on the area now occupied by Bozar.

Charlotte's first sight of the place on 15 February 1842 is

The Palais des Beaux-Arts ('Bozar'); the Brontë Society plaque is above the tiny window to the left of the awning with "BOZAR" on it.

recorded in *The Professor*, the first of her two 'Brussels novels'. It was written soon after she left Belgium but was rejected by publishers and did not see the light of day until after her death. Its setting, like that of her later novel *Villette*, is a school in Brussels closely based on the Pensionnat, but its story is less biographical than *Villette*. For one thing the narrator is a young man, whereas *Villette*'s narrator Lucy Snowe is in many ways a portrait of Charlotte.

The hero, William Crimsworth, arrives in Brussels looking for work, which he is soon to find as a teacher of English. To fill in time before meeting a man who he hopes will help him find a job he goes for a stroll along Rue Royale:

> I saw what a fine street was the Rue Royale, and, walking leisurely along its broad pavement, I continued to survey its stately hotels, till the palisades, the gates, and trees of the park appearing in sight, offered to my eye a new attraction. I remember, before entering the park, I stood awhile to contemplate the statue of General Belliard, and then I advanced to the top of the great staircase just beyond, and

I looked down into a narrow back street, which I afterwards learnt was called the Rue d'Isabelle. I well recollect
that my eye rested on the green door of a rather large house
opposite, where, on a brass plate, was inscribed, 'Pensionnat
de Demoiselles'. (*The Professor*, Chapter 7)

What Charlotte and Emily saw when they went through this
door is graphically recounted in both of Charlotte's 'Brussels
novels'. It is described in most detail in *Villette*, written ten years
after she left Brussels but with total recall of every room in the
school. If we follow Lucy Snowe through the classrooms of
Mme Beck's school we will have a good idea of what life at the
Pensionnat Heger was like for Charlotte and Emily.

Plaque placed by the Brontë Society in
1979 to commemorate Charlotte's and
Emily's stay in Brussels

4

CHARLOTTE AND EMILY
AT THE PENSIONNAT

I don't deny that I sometimes wish to be in England or that I have brief attacks of homesickness – but . . . I have been happy in Brussels because I have always been fully occupied with the employments that I like. (Letter to Ellen Nussey, July 1842)

Emily is making rapid progress in French, German, music and drawing. Monsieur and Madame Heger begin to recognize the valuable points of her character under her singularities. (Letter to Ellen Nussey, July 1842)

If the national character of the Belgians is to be measured by the character of most of the girls in this school . . . their principles are rotten to the core. (Letter to Ellen Nussey, July 1842)

On the Brontës' arrival the 'portress' ('Rosine' in *Villette*) would have taken them into the parlour in the living quarters of Mme Heger, her husband and their three young children. After this first meeting with her they would have been shown round the school. The buildings formed three sides of a quadrangle, and large casement windows opened on to an extensive garden – not visible from the surrounding streets – that occupied quite a lot of the irregular triangle formed by Rue d'Isabelle, Rue Terarken and

Panoramic view of Rue d'Isabelle and the Pensionnat, with the Cathedral
in the background, probably dating from the 1850s
*From Victor Tahon, La rue Isabelle et le Jardin des Arbalétriers,
Rossignol et Van den Bril, Brussels, 1912; Brussels City Archives*

Rue des Douze Apôtres. Downstairs, they would have been shown the three big classrooms and the refectory, which was used not just for meals but also for evening study followed by the *lecture pieuse* deprecated by Charlotte – readings about the lives of saints and martyrs. Upstairs was the long dormitory in which they were to sleep with the other boarders and the oratory, used for the evening prayers which they, as Protestants, were not expected to attend.

In this building Charlotte spent the best part of the next two years and Emily about nine months until she returned to Haworth towards the end of 1842. They studied diligently. They sat in the back row in one of the classrooms, attending the lessons with the other girls. There were around ninety pupils, only some of whom boarded at the school. The Brontës wrote homework assignments, essays, for Monsieur Heger, the headmistress's husband, who taught literature at the school and tutored them in French.

In the dormitory the two sisters, who at twenty-five and twenty-three were much older than the other pupils, were given

Rue d'Isabelle. The photo shows the Pensionnat as it was in the
later nineteenth century when the façade had been rebuilt in a
more uniform style. In the Brontës' time most of the school buildings
were hidden out of sight from the street behind a row of small houses.
These were subsequently acquired by the Hegers and incorporated
into the school building, and the façade was remodelled.
Published in Frederika MacDonald, The Secret of Charlotte Brontë,
T.C. and E.C. Jack, Edinburgh, 1914

a certain amount of privacy by curtains that separated off their
end of the room from the rest. This was emblematic of their position at the school throughout their time there. They were always
together, 'isolated in the midst of numbers', as Charlotte put it
in a letter to her best friend Ellen Nussey,[1] although they were
not the only foreigners studying there. Like expatriates and immi-
grants today who have trouble 'integrating' in the host culture,
they suffered from a fair amount of what is nowadays termed
'culture shock'. It has to be said, though, the Brontë girls suffered
from culture shock in all their encounters with the world outside
their close family unit, whether in England or abroad.

They in fact made no attempt to 'integrate'. They sought
friends only among their English connections in the city. The other
girls found them odd. They were particularly struck by the strange
appearance of Emily who never followed the fashions and favoured
straight skirts and outmoded wide sleeves when the vogue was for

37

the opposite. 'I wish to be as God made me,' she would say in defence of her shapeless dresses.

Emily left no written record of how she felt about her stay in Belgium. She had few correspondents, hardly any of her letters have survived and none of her writings make any direct reference to her time abroad. But we know that she was always miserable away from home. Writing after her sister's death, Charlotte said that Emily failed to adjust to Brussels. 'She was never happy till she carried her hard-won knowledge back to the remote English village, the old parsonage-house, and desolate Yorkshire hills.'[2]

All the lessons were given in French, and Charlotte said that Emily initially struggled to follow them, although her surviving French essays, like Charlotte's, show a competent level in the language. But the Brontës didn't just study French language and literature. Emily had drawing lessons and took advantage of the music teachers available in Brussels to make progress with her piano playing. She also gave piano lessons to some of the younger pupils. She does not seem to have been a popular teacher, though, one reason being that she insisted on giving the lessons during recreation periods so that she could maximize her own study time. One of her piano pupils, however, a girl called Louise De Bassompierre, found Emily more *sympathique* than Charlotte.

Both sisters also took the opportunity to learn some German, probably from a Mlle Mühl who Charlotte mentions in a letter as charging rather high fees for her classes. (Similarly, in *Villette* Lucy and Paulina De Bassompierre learn German together with a Fräulein Braun.) Emily seems to have enjoyed these studies, since back at the Parsonage she would prop her German grammar book in front of her on the kitchen table while kneading the dough for the household's bread.

If Emily left no record of what she thought of the Pensionnat, Charlotte recorded her own feelings about it all too thoroughly. In her letters and novels she hardly had a good word to say about anyone in the school. She was dismissive of Belgians but did not spare other nationalities either. She found both the girls and teachers lacking in principle, feeling and intelligence, insincere, frivolous and dull.

Why did she regard everyone in the place as so despicable, with the exception of herself and Emily and some of the other English pupils? (As we shall see, she also made an exception of M. Heger, the sole man in residence.) Charlotte's analysis was simple. They were foreigners. And Catholics! That explained their lack of every good quality bred into good English Protestants. She saw Catholicism as 'ignorant, unthinking, unquestioning'. At the Pensionnat where Lucy Snowe works in *Villette*, the directress, Mme Beck, is dominated by priests, and the pupils and teachers, in turn, are constantly spied on by her. The pupils are not trusted to behave well of their own volition and not encouraged to think for themselves. What is more, keeping up appearances, *les convenances* (propriety), is seen as more important than having genuinely sound values, going to church more important than telling the truth.

Of course Charlotte did not hold a monopoly on criticizing the people and cultures of other countries, a popular sport in her time and still practised in ours. The Brontës' English friends in Brussels were often just as rude about foreigners. Besides, Charlotte's comments on the pupils and teachers at the schools she had known in England had been no more flattering. And as time went on she became increasingly unhappy in Brussels for reasons that had nothing to do with the character of the Belgians. She was in emotional turmoil, and her view of Belgium and its people was increasingly coloured and twisted by her own private drama.

But at the start of her stay she was very contented. She loved the French language and enjoyed being a pupil again rather than trying to be a teacher. Later on she was to give classes in English at the school to pay for her keep – a less happy experience – but she continued to have tuition in French. As *Villette* shows, she had good times as well as bad within the walls of the Pensionnat, moments of ecstasy as well as misery. *Villette*'s heroine Lucy Snowe has fun observing the school's inmates and customs; Charlotte herself was an inveterate people-watcher. Being in a strange country sharpened her powers of observation. She never tired of watching the odd foreigners and their ways.

And her impressions were certainly not all negative. She acknowledged that life at the Pensionnat was more pleasant than at most English boarding-schools. The directress was a married woman with children – she was pregnant with her fourth when the Brontës arrived – and a husband who was a frequent presence in the classrooms. The fact that the Heger family lived on the premises made the place as much a home as a school. The couple were kind and welcoming to the two sisters from Yorkshire, at least until Charlotte's feelings for the husband complicated her relationship with his wife. The daily routine was much less of a grind than in the schools Charlotte and Emily had known, the worst of which provided the model for Lowood in *Jane Eyre*; there was plenty of recreation time and the classes themselves were not taxing.

Although Charlotte complained in *Villette* that Catholic schools cared more about the pupils' physical well-being than their spiritual welfare, her concern for the souls of those around her did not prevent her from appreciating the amenities provided for the body – starting with the food. Lucy Snowe, arriving cold and hungry at Mme Beck's Pensionnat, falls in love with continental cuisine on her very first evening there. She likes foreign sauces ('odd but pleasant') as much as she dislikes the religion. Belgian fare undoubtedly stimulated the taste buds more than the boiled potatoes and meat served up at the Parsonage. In the Pensionnat the simplest things – *tartines* (slices of bread and butter) or the breakfast *pistolets* (rolls) – were tasty. Charlotte had a sweet tooth; similarly Lucy adores pears from the Pensionnat garden stewed in white wine, and Crimsworth in *The Professor* buys himself one of the buns known as *couques* (from the Flemish *koek*) still ubiquitous in Brussels cake shops today. M. Heger is known to have carried sweets in his pockets to reward his pupils, and the fictional hero inspired by him, M. Paul in *Villette*, does not nourish Lucy's mind alone; he feeds her with cream cakes after banishing her to the attic to learn her lines

The Pensionnat and its garden. This photo was taken after the Brontës'
time. The *galerie* with arched windows was added in 1857.
Brontë Parsonage Museum

for the school play, and as they get to know each other they bond
over shared brioches.

Charlotte also seems to have enjoyed as much as anyone else
the festivals punctuating the Catholic year and the theatrical pro-
ductions and dances and outings to the countryside that made the
terms pass pleasantly. While criticizing these regular distractions
from the school routine as an attempt to 'hide with flowers' the
'chains' of a religion that demanded unthinking obedience rather
than individual responsibility, in *Villette* she records with affection
rites such as the bouquets of flowers presented to M. Paul on his
saint's day or *fête*.

In summer a lot of time was spent in the garden that gave
the Pensionnat so much of its charm. It must have been as welcome
to Charlotte and Emily as Mme Beck's garden is to Lucy Snowe.
Instead of the rambles on the moors they were used to, much of
their exercise in Brussels was taken in this walled garden, but,
confined as it was, it fired Charlotte's imagination. It was a secret,
hidden place. As the year turned to spring, girls and teachers alike
spent more and more time in this oasis in the middle of the busy

city, with its *berceaux* (arbours covered in vines), its row of pear trees and the Allée Défendue ('forbidden walk'), the path that was out of bounds to the demoiselles because on the other side of the garden wall was a boys' school, the Athénée Royal, where M. Heger also taught. Here Charlotte and Emily would walk separately from the other girls, Emily leaning on her sister despite being much taller than the tiny Charlotte.

Thus, life at the Pensionnat, at least initially, offered plenty of new sensations and impressions. And although Charlotte's comments on Belgians often sound like those of any grumpy foreigner abroad, convinced that everything is better back home, her stay there changed her for ever.

Of all the influences on her at the Pensionnat, the most important was her charismatic teacher, Constantin Heger.

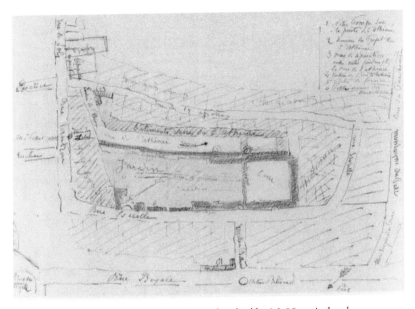

Rough plan of the Pensionnat area sketched by M. Heger's daughter
Louise after the demolition of the school. Louise's sketch shows the
Pensionnat, with its *cour* (quadrangle/playground) and garden, together
with the adjoining Athénée at a lower level, lying in the area formed by
Rue d'Isabelle, Rue Terarken and Rue des Douze Apôtres. The buildings
underwent many changes, and the drawing reflects the school as it was
after the Brontës' time, including the *galerie* forming the fourth side of the
playground built in the 1850s. However, the plan shows the basic layout
of the school they knew, with the main entrance directly opposite the
Belliard steps and the Hegers' living quarters on the left. It also shows the
chief features of the garden – the Allée Défendue and *grand berceau* skirting
the wall dividing the two schools, the pear-tree walk down the middle
of the garden and, at the bottom left-hand corner, the old gateway
(*porte monumentale*).
Brontë Parsonage Museum

Opposite: Population census for 1842, listing Charlotte and Emily Brontë
(spelled 'Bronti') among the inmates of the Pensionnat Heger at No. 32
Rue d'Isabelle. Near the top of the page are Constantin Heger and
Zoë Claire Heger (née Parent) and their children at the time,
Marie, Louise and Claire.
Brussels City Archives

I WISH I DID KNOW WHOM!

Lucy Snowe musing on the provenance of a love letter she finds in the
Allée Défendue in the garden of Mme Beck's Pensionnat
Edmund Dulac, illustration for Villette, Dent, London, *1922*

5

MONSIEUR HEGER

A dark little man he certainly was; pungent and austere. Even to me he seemed a harsh apparition, with his close-shorn, black head, his broad, sallow brow, his thin cheek, his wide and quivering nostril, his thorough glance and hurried bearing. Irritable he was; one heard that, as he apostrophized with vehemence the awkward squad under his orders. Sometimes he would break out on these raw amateur actresses with a passion of impatience at their falseness of conception, their coldness of emotion, their feebleness of delivery. (Lucy Snowe observes M. Paul rehearsing the pupils for the school play in *Villette*, Chapter 14)

He fumed like a bottled storm. (*Villette*, Chapter 15)

He broke in two the 'brioche,' intended for his own refreshment, and gave me half. Truly his bark was worse than his bite . . . (*Villette*, Chapter 30)

Well might we like him, with all his passions and hurricanes, when he could be so benignant and docile at times, as he was just now. (*Villette*, Chapter 33)

The 'Pensionnat Heger-Parent' had been started by Zoë Parent some years before she married Constantin Heger. At the time the Brontës arrived, the couple had been married for five years and

The Heger family in 1846, by Ange François. By 1846 the family of six
children was complete. All except the youngest, Paul, had been born by the
time Charlotte left Brussels. Paul, here a babe in arms, became a scientist
and the most distinguished of the Hegers' offspring. Louise, in a straw hat,
became a successful artist. Charlotte always remembered her fondly and is
thought to have depicted her as little Georgette in *Villette*.
Reproduced by kind permission of the owner

had three children; two more were born during Charlotte's stay. Madame was thirty-seven, her husband thirty-three.

Zoë Claire Parent, an attractive woman and efficient manager, had everything Charlotte coveted: looks, fulfilling employment and happiness in her personal life. What Charlotte must have come to envy her for more than anything else was that she had Constantin Heger.

It was his second marriage. He had lost his first wife and the only child of that marriage to a cholera epidemic. Before settling down as a schoolmaster he had had quite an eventful youth; when his jeweller father lost a lot of money through an imprudent loan, Constantin, then only a teenager, went to seek his fortune in Paris: he worked as secretary to a solicitor and dreamed of becoming a lawyer himself but had to relinquish the idea because of lack of funds. He soon returned to Belgium, and as a young man of twenty-one fought in the 1830 revolution. But by the time the Brontës knew him he had been teaching for several years both at the Pensionnat and at the Athénée next door and had established a reputation as an inspirational schoolmaster.

He obviously made a strong impression on Charlotte from their first encounter. She accused Belgians of being so phlegmatic that 'the phlegm that thickens their blood is too gluey to boil'.[1] M. Heger must have been a notable exception; he always seemed to be at boiling point and in her descriptions sounds more like a fiery Italian than a Belgian, although his family actually originated from Germany. (Transformed into the passionate M. Paul, he is given a swarthy complexion and 'Spanish blood'.) Her first reference to him in a letter appears highly uncomplimentary. He is 'a little, black, ugly being' and she compares his facial expression when angry to that of 'an insane tom-cat' or 'delirious hyena'.[2] But Charlotte often used such immoderate language about people who in fact intrigued and attracted her. Clearly he suited the passionate temperament of a Brontë. And he was the inspiration for more than one of her literary heroes. The moody Mr Rochester in *Jane Eyre* surely owes something to Monsieur Heger — apart from the obvious circumstance that both men were, inconveniently, married!

In her letters and in *Villette* we can trace how the fascination she felt for the man she called her 'master' became an obsession that was to dominate her for years.

His method of tutoring the two sisters was to read them passages from the French writers he admired, get them to analyse the style and then set them essays in French on similar subjects. They had been writing obsessively for years, but their extravagantly romantic stories had been undirected and uncorrected by any adult. Heger, however, insisted on the need for imitation, knowledge and discipline as well as inspiration. He edited what they wrote, rendering their style more precise and terse, rejecting what he found irrelevant: '*Remorselessly* sacrifice everything that does not contribute to clarity, verisimilitude, and effect... accentuate everything that sets the main idea in relief...'.[3] He rewrote passages, while at the same time appreciating and nurturing their talent. Charlotte, at least, left Belgium a better writer; there is a quantum leap between her self-indulgent juvenile scribblings and the novels she produced after her time in Brussels.

She relished writing French essays for Heger as a means of impressing him and also of entering into a dialogue with him, for example, when debating the respective importance, for a writer, of inspiration ('genius') and of craftsmanship. She always championed the former, Heger the latter. In 'An Essay on Style: The Fall of the Leaves' (30 March 1843), which took as its starting-point reflections on the poem 'La Chute des Feuilles' by Charles-Hubert Millevoye, she wrote:

> I believe that all true poetry is but the faithful imprint of something that happens or has happened in the poet's soul . . . To write a . . . poem like 'The Fall of the Leaves', does one need anything other than genius cooperating with a feeling, an affection, or a passion of some kind? . . .
> I believe that genius, thus awakened, has no need to seek

the details, that it scarcely pauses to reflect . . . I believe that
the details come quite naturally without the poet's seeking
them, that inspiration takes the place of reflection.[4]

Heger's corrections and comments can be read on the manuscripts of the essays. Commenting on this one, he wrote:

Man knows not what genius is; it is a gift from Heaven, it is
something divine . . . It is the same with force. But imagine
two men of equal strength, one without a lever, the other
with a lever. The first will lift 1,000 pounds, the second, in
making the same effort, will uproot a tree. Is the lever nothing? Without the voice, no singer – doubtless; but no singer
either without craft, without study, without imitation . . .
    Without study, no art . . . art epitomizes that which all the
centuries bequeath to us, all that man has found beautiful, that
which has had an effect on man, all that he has found worth
saving from oblivion. Genius, without study and without art,
without the knowledge of what has been done, is force without
the lever . . . it is the sublime musician . . . who has only an
untuned piano to make the world hear the dulcet melodies
that he hears reverberating inwardly.[5]

That Charlotte partially conceded his point can be seen from her
essay 'Letter from a Poor Painter' following this chapter.

Whether M. Heger had any influence on Emily is less easy to
ascertain. She rebelled against his teaching methods. Originality, not imitation, was what she valued in writing. Heger was critical of her
unwillingness to compromise and admit other points of view but
acknowledged the force of her intellect. He told Charlotte's biographer
Elizabeth Gaskell that Emily 'should have been a man. She had a head
for logic, and a capability of argument, unusual in a man, and rare indeed
in a woman.'[6]

We can judge the immediate effect of his teaching in the thirty
or so essays or *devoirs* (homework assignments) that Charlotte and Emily

Manuscript page of Charlotte Brontë's 'La Chute des feuilles'
Reproduced by kind permission of François Fierens

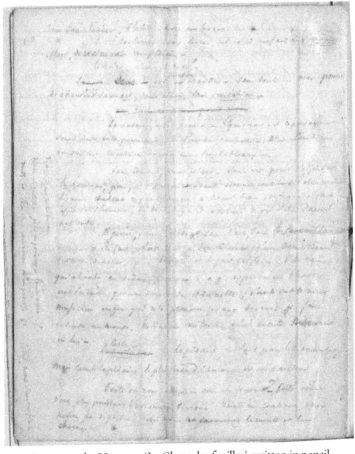

Comments by Heger on 'La Chute des feuilles', written in pencil
Reproduced by kind permission of François Fierens

wrote for him on topics such as 'The Death of Napoleon', 'The Aim of Life' and 'The Caterpillar', even if they did not always develop their subjects as he might have foreseen: for example, Charlotte manages to transform her essay on Napoleon into a eulogy of her hero Wellington.

The collected *devoirs* have been published as 'the Belgian essays', with English translations and Heger's amendments and comments. The manuscripts themselves, like all the Brontë manuscripts, are scattered far and wide. Many ended up in America. M. Heger sometimes gave them as souvenirs to the American literary pilgrims who regularly rang the bell of the Pensionnat hoping for a glimpse of Lucy Snowe's school. He held on to a handful of them, and four are still in Brussels, in the possession of one of his descendants. And in 2011 a *devoir* turned up in the Mariemont Museum in southern Belgium. It had disappeared from sight in 1915 when Heger's son Paul gave it to a wealthy magnate for his manuscript collection, which was later left to the Belgian state.

Whatever Heger may have thought of the way in which Charlotte and Emily – particularly Emily – sometimes chose to develop the topics he set them, their essays trace their remarkable progress in French under his eye. Charlotte's love of the language – the year after leaving Brussels she was thrilled to have an opportunity of conversing with a French or Belgian gentleman she met on a train – found its way into all four of her novels, even those not set in Brussels. She introduces French speakers both into *Jane Eyre* (Mr Rochester's little ward Adèle) and *Shirley* (the half-Belgian hero Robert Gérard Moore, his brother Louis and sister Hortense).

An important reason for her love of French was that it was the language of M. Heger. It is not surprising that she enjoyed being tutored by him. His charisma is conveyed powerfully in the character of M. Paul. He had a huge love of language and literature and could engage with Charlotte and Emily intellectually, but equally attractive for Charlotte was his personality. Like many inspiring teachers he was eccentric and temperamental. The storms that erupted when he lost his temper and made his pupils cry for failing to live up to his expectations alternated with the sunny spells of his more benevolent humours.

Charlotte's account of the volatile master is borne out by those of other ex-pupils. One of these, Frederika Macdonald, wrote about her years at the Pensionnat from 1859 to 1861 in her book *The Secret of Charlotte Brontë*. She did not altogether hit it off with M. Heger, and her picture of him does not match Charlotte's in all points; perhaps it gives a clearer-eyed view of him. Inspiring though he was as a literature teacher, she found him less lovable and less interesting intellectually than Charlotte's M. Paul. To her he seemed a man who saw 'the world as his classroom' and 'told people what they ought to think',[7] using maxims to convince his hearers rather than engaging in argument. But in her encounters with him we catch many glimpses of M. Paul, whether reducing a class of girls to tears and then beaming on them benignly (he was put out when Frederika refused to weep) or, in a one-to-one tutorial, demonstrating an arithmetic problem with a macaroon biscuit before sharing it with the struggling pupil. We see him inveigling Frederika, when he bumps into her in the garden, into helping him to wash his dog in the cigar-scented library and rewarding her with a book.

Heger had great histrionic talent, and the frequency of tears in classes over which he presided was owing to the way he worked on his pupils' emotions to make them more receptive to the beauties of literature. An ex-pupil recalled that on one occasion when a class of girls proved unresponsive their frustrated teacher became increasingly overwrought until finally, to everyone's astonishment, he burst into tears himself and made an abrupt exit.

Despite his eccentricities he was in many ways conventional – a family man, a bourgeois, a pillar of society, a devout Catholic. He and his wife were highly respected figures in the city, and many of the best families sent their daughters to be educated by them.

At one stage during her second year at the Pensionnat Charlotte and Heger reversed roles. She became the teacher and he the pupil. She taught him English for a time and was amused by his efforts to master English pronunciation. This was probably Charlotte's most enjoyable – perhaps her only enjoyable – experience of teaching.

Contact with him rapidly became the most important thing in her life. But this happy phase in their relationship was not to last. Most of her second year at the school, when Emily was no longer with her, was a much more sombre period in her Brussels experience.

In *Villette*, a novel as dark in parts as that lonely second year, but illuminated by the sparks flying between Lucy and M. Paul, Charlotte imagined a different and happier development of her relationship with Heger.

But before seeing how he was transmuted into M. Paul by her imagination, let us read some of the essays written for the real Heger.

6

FOUR DEVOIRS BY CHARLOTTE AND EMILY

These English translations of the essays are taken from Sue Lonoff (ed.),
The Belgian Essays: A Critical Edition, *Yale University Press, 1996,*
with the exception of 'L'Ingratitude', which did not come to light until 2011.
The translation of the latter essay is also by Sue Lonoff.

'The Cat' by Emily Brontë
15 May 1842

In this defence of cats, while admitting the common view of them as
self-interested, hypocritical and cruel, Emily argues that in this they are
no different from human beings. (Her concluding remark relates to the
belief held by some doctrines that animals, like humans, were originally
good but were expelled from Paradise.)

I can say with sincerity that I like cats; also I can give very good reasons why those who despise them are wrong.

A cat is an animal who has more human feelings than almost any other being. We cannot sustain a comparison with the dog, it is infinitely too good; but the cat, although it differs in some physical points, is extremely like us in disposition.

There may be people, in truth, who would say that this resemblance extends only to the most wicked men; that it is limited to their excessive hypocrisy, cruelty, and ingratitude; detestable vices in our race and equally odious in that of cats.

Without disputing the limits that those individuals set on our affinity, I answer that if hypocrisy, cruelty and ingratitude are exclusively the domain of the wicked, that class comprises everyone. Our education develops one of those qualities in great perfection; the others flourish without nurture, and far from condemning them, we regard all three with great complacency. A cat, in its own interest, sometimes hides its misanthropy under the guise of amiable gentleness; instead of tearing what it desires from its master's hand, it approaches with a caressing air, rubs its pretty little head against him, and advances a paw whose touch is soft as down. When it has gained its end, it resumes its character of Timon; and that artfulness in it is called hypocrisy. In ourselves, we give it another name, politeness, and he who did not use it to hide his real feelings would soon be driven from society.

'But', says some delicate lady, who has murdered a half-dozen lapdogs through pure affection, 'the cat is such a cruel beast, he is not content to kill his prey, he torments it before its death; you cannot make that accusation against us.' More or less, Madame. Your husband, for example, likes hunting very much, but foxes being rare on his land, he would not have the means to pursue this amusement often, if he did not manage his supplies thus: once he has run an animal to its last breath, he snatches it from the jaws of the hounds and saves it to suffer the same infliction two or three more times, ending finally in death. You yourself avoid a bloody spectacle because it wounds your weak nerves. But I have seen you embrace your child in transports, when he came to show you a beautiful butterfly crushed between his cruel little fingers; and at that moment, I really wanted to have a cat, with the tail of a half-devoured rat hanging from its mouth, to present as the image, the true copy, of your angel. You could not refuse to kiss him, and if he scratched us both in revenge, so much the better. Little boys are rather liable to acknowledge their friends' caresses in that way, and the resemblance would be more perfect. The ingratitude of cats is another name for penetration. They know how to value our favours at their true price, because they guess the motives that prompt us to grant them, and if those motives might sometimes be good, undoubtedly they remember always that they owe all their misery and all their evil qualities to the great ancestor of humankind. For assuredly, the cat was not wicked in Paradise.

'The Butterfly' by Emily Brontë
11 August 1842

The narrator begins in pessimistic mood, seeing a caterpillar destroying a flower as a symbol of the principle governing a world in which every living thing destroys and is destroyed. But the sight of a butterfly brings a vision of a better world beyond, in which our suffering in this one will be understood as part of God's plan.

In one of those moods that everyone falls into sometimes, when the world of the imagination suffers a winter that blights its vegetation; when the light of life seems to go out and existence becomes a barren desert where we wander, exposed to all the tempests that blow under heaven, without hope of rest or shelter – in one of these black humours, I was walking one evening at the edge of a forest. It was summer; the sun was still shining high in the west and the air resounded with the songs of birds. All appeared happy, but for me, it was only an appearance. I sat at the foot of an old oak, among whose branches the nightingale had just begun its vespers. 'Poor fool,' I said to myself, 'is it to guide the bullet to your breast or the child to your brood that you sing so loud and clear? Silence that untimely tune, perch yourself on your nest; tomorrow, perhaps, it will be empty.' But why address myself to you alone? All creation is equally mad. Behold those flies playing above the brook; the swallows and fish diminish their number every minute. These will become, in their turn, the prey of some tyrant of the air or water; and man for his amusement or his needs will kill their murderers.

Nature is an inexplicable problem; it exists on a principle of destruction. Every being must be the tireless instrument of death to others, or itself must cease to live, yet nonetheless we celebrate the day of our birth, and we praise God for having entered such a world.

During my soliloquy I picked a flower at my side; it was fair and freshly opened, but an ugly caterpillar had hidden itself among the petals and already they were shrivelling and fading. 'Sad image of the earth and its inhabitants!' I exclaimed. 'This worm lives only to injure the plant that protects it. Why was it created, and why was man created? He torments, he kills, he devours; he suffers, dies, is devoured — there you have his whole story. It is true that there is a heaven for the saint, but the saint leaves enough misery here below to sadden him even before the throne of God.'

I threw the flower to earth. At that moment the universe appeared to me a vast machine constructed only to produce evil. I almost doubted the goodness of God, in not annihilating man on the day he first sinned. 'The world should have been destroyed,' I said, 'crushed as I crush this reptile which has done nothing in its life but render all that it touches as disgusting as itself.' I had scarcely removed my foot from the poor insect when, like a censoring angel sent from heaven, there came fluttering through the trees a butterfly with large wings of lustrous gold and purple. It shone but a moment before my eyes; then, rising among the leaves, it vanished into the height of the azure vault. I was mute, but an inner voice said to me, 'Let not the creature judge his Creator; here is a symbol of the world to come. As the ugly caterpillar is the origin of the splendid butterfly, so this globe is the embryo of a new heaven and a new earth whose poorest beauty will infinitely exceed your mortal imagination. And when you see the magnificent result of that which seems so base to you now, how you will scorn your blind presumption, in accusing Omniscience for not having made nature perish in her infancy.'

God is the god of justice and mercy; then surely, every grief that he inflicts on his creatures, be they human or animal, rational or

Manuscript page of a *devoir* called 'Ma chère Maman' by Emily Brontë
Reproduced by kind permission of François Fierens

irrational, every suffering of our unhappy nature is only a seed of that divine harvest which will be gathered when, Sin having spent its last drop of venom, Death having launched its final shaft, both will perish on the pyre of a universe in flames and leave their ancient victims to an eternal empire of happiness and glory.

'Ingratitude' by Charlotte Brontë
16 March 1842

The first extant devoir *by Charlotte. It disappeared from view in 1915 and was rediscovered in 2011 in a Belgian museum. It was probably inspired by fables such as those of La Fontaine.*

A rat, weary of the life of cities, and of courts (for he had played his part in the palaces of kings and in the salons of great lords), a rat whom experience had made wise, in short, a rat who from a courtier had become a philosopher, had withdrawn to his country house (a hole in the trunk of a large young elm), where he lived as a hermit devoting all his time and care to the education of his only son.

The young rat, who had not yet received those severe but salutary lessons that experience gives, was a bit thoughtless; the wise counsels of his father seemed boring to him; the shade and tranquillity of the woods, instead of calming his mind, tired him. He grew impatient to travel and see the world.

One fine morning, he arose early, he made up a little packet of cheese and grains, and without saying a word to anyone, the ingrate abandoned his father and his paternal abode and departed for lands unknown.

At first all seemed charming to him; the flowers were of a fresh-ness, the trees of a greenness that he had never seen at home – and then, he saw so many wonders: an animal with a tail larger than its body (it was a squirrel), a little creature that carried its house on its back (it was a snail). After several hours he approached a farm, the smell of cooking attracted him, he entered the farmyard – there he saw a kind of gigantic bird who was making a horrible noise as he marched with an air fierce and proud. Now, this bird was a turkey, but our rat took him for a monster, and frightened by his aspect, he immediately fled.

Towards evening, he entered a wood, weary and tired he sat down at the foot of a tree, he opened his little packet, ate his supper, and went to bed.

Waking with the lark he felt his limbs numbed by the cold, his hard bed hurt him; then he remembered his father, the ingrate recalled the care and tenderness of the good old rat, he formed vain resolutions for the future, but it was too late, the cold had frozen his blood. Experience was for him an austere mistress, she gave him but one lesson and one punishment; it was death.

The next day a woodcutter found the corpse, he saw it only as something disgusting – and pushed it with his foot in passing, without thinking that there lay the ungrateful son of a tender father.

Extract from 'Letter from a Poor Painter to a Great Lord' by Charlotte Brontë
17 October 1843

This is the last of Charlotte's French essays, a letter to a potential patron by a young painter, 'George Howard'. He recounts that he became an artist from a sense of vocation and a conviction of his own genius, 'a force within'. Since childhood he has been aware of his difference from others – he feels things too deeply, is excessive in everything he does – as well as his physical unattractiveness. He finds consolation in Nature for his social failure until, tiring of a contemplative life, he resolves to make his way in the world and goes to Italy to learn his craft, beavering away as determinedly as Charlotte in Brussels. It is not difficult to see much of Charlotte herself in her imaginary painter, twenty-five years old and alone in a foreign country. As well as revealing her character and ambition to Heger, she pursues their ongoing debate on the roles of inspiration or genius, on the one hand, and discipline, knowledge, craftsmanship, on the other. In this last essay for him, while insisting that great art can be created only by genius – something that cannot be taught – she acknowledges that it must be accompanied by technical skill, acquired through hard work. After an introductory paragraph her painter pens a self-portrait.

I am, Milord, a twenty-five-year-old man who has chosen to become a painter, who has just completed his studies in Rome, who arrives in this country without acquaintances and without family, and who has no other fortune than his palette, his paintbrushes, his craftsmanship, and the love of his art. Such is my position; I know how hazardous, how suspect, even how contemptible it is in the eyes of certain people who regard as shameful everything that is perilous and uncertain. Why then have I chosen a career whose dangers I know so well? What right have I to hope to succeed where so many others have succumbed? Milord, I shall answer these questions, and frankly. I entered upon this career because I believed that it was my vocation; I hope to succeed in it because I sense in myself the courage to persevere despite all the obstacles I may encounter. These are not the words of a braggart who thinks himself brave because he has never been put to the test; I know what misfortune is; I have suffered it in its harshest forms. The four years that I spent in Italy were not exclusively devoted to the study of the arts; I had also to take my degree in the school of Adversity, and if I did not sink under the severity of its discipline, it is because the love of my art was in me a passion that rekindled the fire in my veins when cold and hunger had frozen them. 'But', you would say, 'the love of your art is nothing if you do not have the talent necessary to attain excellence in it.' Milord, I believe I have talent. Do not be indignant at my presumption or accuse me of conceit; I do not know that feeble feeling, the child of vanity; but I know well another feeling, respect for myself, a feeling born of independence and integrity. Milord, I believe I have Genius.

That declaration shocks you, you find it arrogant; I find it very simple. Doesn't everyone agree that no artist can succeed without genius? Then would it not be imbecility to dedicate oneself to the arts without being sure one has that indispensable quality? But how to acquire that assurance? Can one not be mistaken about it? Man is so inclined to flatter himself. I know only one sure method. One must live in the world, compare oneself with others, submit oneself to the test of experience, pass through its furnace, ten times fiercer than Nebuchadnezzar's, and if one emerges from it without being transmuted into the ordinary lead of society, it is because one's soul contains a few grains of that pure gold which is called Genius. Milord, I lived for a long time with others without any thought of comparing myself with them; throughout my early youth the difference that existed between myself and most of the people around me was, for me, an embarrassing enigma that I did not know how to resolve. I believed myself inferior to everyone, and it grieved me. I believed it my duty to follow the example set by most of my acquaintances, an example sanctioned by the approbation of legitimate and prudent mediocrity, yet all the while I felt myself incapable of feeling and acting as they felt and acted. Say one of my comrades performed some feat and he was applauded; I imitated him and I was scolded. People found me always clumsy, always boring. There was always excess in what I did; I was either too wrought up or too cast down; without meaning to, I showed everything that passed in my heart, and sometimes storms were passing through it. In vain I tried to imitate the gentle gaiety, the serene and even temper, that I saw in the faces of my companions and found so worthy of admiration; all my efforts were useless. I could not restrain the ebb and flow of blood in my arteries, and that ebb and flow left its mark upon my physiognomy and upon my harsh and unengaging features; I cried in secret. Finally, a day came (I was eighteen) when I opened my eyes and glimpsed a heaven in my own soul. Suddenly I realized that I had a force within that could serve as a substitute for that noble calm which I had so much admired: I discovered that the heart holds certain things called feelings; I felt that those feelings were alive and deep within my nature, and that they were soon to make me both slave and master of all that pleases, animates, touches us in this glorious Creation; slave, because I was subjugated by it to the point of prostration, master because I knew how to draw inexpressible delight from it at will. I had loved society, and society had coldly rejected me; now I loved Nature, and she sweetly unveiled her face to me and let me imbibe the calm of happiness in the contemplation of her divine features. I thought I no longer needed mankind; I had found friends in the desert and in the forest. The simplest things gave me genuine pleasure. It took no more than an old oak with a mossy trunk, with twisted branches, than a bubbling spring bordered with wild flowers, than the ivy-coloured ruins of a tower bristling with brambles and thorns, to throw me into the most exquisite transports of the soul. I became a painter and a dreamer.

At twenty-one my dreams dissipated. I do not know what voice it was that cried in my ear, 'Rouse yourself! leave your world of phantoms, enter the real world, look for Work, confront Experience, struggle and conquer!' I arose, I wrenched myself away from that solitude, those dreams that I loved, I left my country and went abroad.

When I disembarked on the shores of Italy a light seemed to fall upon my future; I saw it full of uncertainty but also full of hope. It stretched before me like a large and uncultivated field. I knew that wheat was not sprouting in it yet, but already I was dreaming of the harvest. I lacked neither courage nor fortitude; immediately I set to work. Sometimes, it is true, despair overwhelmed me for an instant, for when I saw the works of the great masters of my art I felt myself only too contemptible; but the fever of emulation came to drive away that momentary prostration and from that deep consciousness of inferiority, I derived new energy for work; there was born in me a fixed resolution: 'I will do all, suffer all, in order to win all.' And so I suffered much in Florence, in Venice and in Rome, and in those places I won what I wished to possess: an intimate knowledge of all the technical mysteries of Painting, a taste cultivated in accord with the rules of art. As for natural genius, neither Titian nor Raphael nor Michelangelo would have known how to give me that which comes from God alone; the little I have, I possess from my Creator, and within my soul I carefully guard that one drop of the river of life which Mercy has poured out to sweeten so much bitterness: I believe I make good use of it in employing it to add something to the pure pleasures of my fellow men.

Milord, it is to put myself in a position to exercise that faculty that I entreat your help; I could begin my career alone, but then I would still have to work for many years in obscurity and indigence. I know that in the long run true merit always triumphs, but if power does not offer a helping hand, the day of success can be a long time in coming. Sometimes, indeed, death precedes victory, and what is the good of throwing laurels on a grave?

Milord, excuse me if this letter seems long to you. I did not think to count the lines; I thought only of speaking to you sincerely.

Milord, I am

Your obedient servant,

George Howard

But now we leave these essays, written in a language not her own in Charlotte's years of apprenticeship as a writer, for Villette, *the novel of her maturity that revisited her years at the Pensionnat and her contact with Heger.*

"Currer Bell's Pear-tree Garden"; artist's impression of
the Pensionnat garden
Illustration for the article 'Vagabondizing in Belgium', Harper's Monthly *magazine,*
August 1858

7

LUCY SNOWE'S PENSIONNAT

I was sitting on the hidden seat [in the garden] . . .
listening to what seemed the far-off sounds of the city.
Far off, in truth, they were not: this school was in the
city's centre; hence, it was but five minutes' walk to the
park, scarce ten to buildings of palatial splendour. Quite
near were wide streets brightly lit, teeming at this
moment with life: carriages were rolling through them,
to balls or to the opera. The same hour which tolled
curfew for our convent, which extinguished each lamp,
and dropped the curtain round each couch, rung for
the gay city about us the summons to festal enjoyment.
(*Villette*, Chapter 12)

In winter I sought the long classes, and paced them fast
to keep myself warm . . . In summer it was never quite
dark, and then I went up stairs to my own quarter of
the long dormitory, opened my own casement . . . and
leaning out, looked forth upon the city beyond the
garden, and listened to band-music from the park or
the palace-square, thinking meantime my own thoughts,
living my own life in my own still, shadow-world. (*Villette*,
Chapter 13)

'I was conscious of rapport between you and myself.
You are patient, and I am choleric; you are quiet and pale,
and I am tanned and fiery; you are a strict Protestant,

and I am a sort of lay Jesuit: but we are alike – there is affinity. Do you see it, mademoiselle, when you look in the glass? Do you observe that your forehead is shaped like mine – that your eyes are cut like mine? Do you hear that you have some of my tones of voice? Do you know that you have many of my looks? I perceive all this, and believe that you were born under my star. Yes, you were born under my star! Tremble! for where that is the case with mortals, the threads of their destinies are difficult to disentangle; knottings and catchings occur – sudden breaks leave damage in the web.' (M. Paul addressing Lucy in *Villette*, Chapter 31)

'Will Miss Lucy be the sister of a very poor, fettered, burdened, encumbered man?' (*Villette*, Chapter 35)

I envied no girl her lover, no bride her bridegroom, no wife her husband. (*Villette*, Chapter 35, after M. Paul asks Lucy to be his friend)

Lucy Snowe's Pensionnat is in all essentials the Pensionnat Heger as seen by Charlotte. Many aspects of the teachers and pupils of the real Pensionnat are incorporated into characters in the novel. M. Paul Emanuel is of course partly inspired by Constantin Heger, and *Villette* gives a very good idea of what it must have been like being taught by him. Zoë Heger fared less well in Charlotte's version of her, assuming that Charlotte did have her in mind for Lucy's employer Mme Beck, who, cold, calculating and unscrupulous, spies, lies and subjects everyone under her to constant surveillance.

It is possible that some of the traits actually observed by Charlotte in her employer found their way into Mme Beck and also into Zoraïde Reuter, the directress of the girls' school in *The Professor* – apparently 'sensible, sagacious, affable' but in reality hypocritical and ruthless. However, by most accounts the real woman genuinely possessed the admirable qualities that in them were no more than skin deep.

Written a decade after Charlotte's time at the Pensionnat, *Villette* shows how deeply it was etched in her memory. She remembers every detail of every room that provides the backdrop for the unfolding drama of Lucy's emotions, as her passion for the handsome young English doctor 'Dr John' (John Graham Bretton), dominating the first half of the novel, is gradually replaced by the burgeoning relationship with M. Paul – Charlotte's imaginative reworking of her real-life relationship with Heger.

Sometimes this drama is enacted in rooms full of pupils and teachers, as Lucy and Paul Emanuel spar with each other and advance along the tortuous path to mutual understanding in crowded classrooms or in the refectory where the girls sit sewing at two long tables at the end of the day. Preparing to read aloud to them one evening, he thinks Lucy is snubbing him because she moves aside as he seats himself by her. In revenge, he makes all the girls crowd together at one of the tables, placing himself and Lucy at opposite ends of the other one. When annoyed he has no scruples about throwing dignity to the winds and often comes across as childish and absurd. But his fits of pique are endearing because what is behind them is his wish for Lucy to like him and because the essential person underneath is kind and generous. There is the occasion when Lucy interrupts a class to give him a message when he is in a particularly bad mood. The interruption does nothing to improve his humour, and she is so nervous that while handing him the note she accidentally knocks his spectacles off the desk, breaking them. To her relief he turns it into a joke to spare her feelings.

At other times we see Lucy alone in a deserted room while the rest of the school is at play or at prayer. The loneliness Charlotte felt so often amid the bustle of the school and the big city pervades the whole novel. Lucy paces the empty classrooms at dusk, hearing not far away the carriages in Rue Royale taking people to dances or the theatre while she is immured in her 'convent'. She sits alone with her thoughts in the dormitory. (But even with the other girls around her she is an isolated figure, opening the dormitory window, in true Brontëan fashion, to revel in one of Villette's violent thunder storms and leaning out into the night to enjoy it while the terrified girls say prayers.) The place where she is most sure of being alone is in the attic where she hides to read letters from Graham Bretton. It is here that she has one of several sightings of the ghostly nun who haunts the school.

As at the Pensionnat Heger, through the casement windows of Mme Beck's school we are always aware of the garden with its ancient pear tree, 'Methusaleh', at whose foot Lucy buries Graham's letters when she gives up all hope of his love. It is a romantic place into which *billets-doux*, love letters, are thrown over the wall from nearby buildings by lovesick young men and where Lucy has occasional glimpses of the alarming nun. She walks alone there in the cool of the evening, or falls into conversation with M. Paul as he smokes his cigars. Their rambles are similar to those taken in the grounds of Thornfield Hall by Jane and Rochester, another cigar smoker. On summer evenings the action shifts from the classrooms to the tree-lined paths outside as Lucy's and Paul Emanuel's feelings deepen into love and Charlotte's imagination transports the Belgian schoolmaster on whom his character was originally based into the realm of wish-fulfilment.

8

EXTRACT FROM VILLETTE (I)

Lucy Receives a Letter from Graham Bretton and M. Paul Is Not Pleased

Abridged from Chapter 21 of Villette

One afternoon . . . on my way to the first class, where I was expected to assist at a lesson of 'style and literature', I saw . . . Rosine, the portress. Her attitude, as usual, was quite nonchalante . . . One of her hands rested in her apron-pocket, the other, at this moment, held to her eyes a letter, whereof Mademoiselle coolly perused the address, and deliberately studied the seal.

A letter! The shape of a letter similar to that had haunted my brain in its very core for seven days past. I had dreamed of a letter last night . . . (But I heard) the rapid step of the Professor of Literature measuring the corridor. I fled before him . . . I had time to get seated . . . ere M. Emanuel entered . . .

As usual he broke upon us like a clap of thunder; but instead of flashing lightning-wise from the door to the estrade, his career halted midway at my desk. Setting his face towards me and the window, his back to the pupils and the room, he gave me a look – such a look as might have licensed me to stand straight up and demand what he meant – a look of scowling distrust.

'Voilà! pour vous,'[1] said he, drawing his hand from his waist-coat, and placing on my desk a letter – the very letter I had seen in Rosine's hand . . . I knew it, I felt it to be the letter of my hope, the

I SAW, STANDING BY ONE OF THE LONG
AND LARGE WINDOWS, ROSINE,
THE PORTRESS

Edmund Dulac, illustration for Villette, *Dent, London, 1922*

fruition of my wish, the release from my doubt, the ransom from my terror. This letter M. Paul, with his unwarrantably interfering habits, had taken from the portress, and now delivered it himself.

I might have been angry, but had not a second for the sensation. Yes: I held in my hand not a slight note, but an envelope, which must, at least, contain a sheet: it felt, not flimsy, but firm, substantial, satisfying. And here was the direction, 'Miss Lucy Snowe', in a clean, clear, equal, decided hand; and there was the seal . . . stamped with the well-cut impress of initials, 'J. G. B.' I experienced a happy feeling – a glad emotion which went warm to my heart, and ran lively through all my veins. For once a hope was realized. I held in my hand a morsel of real solid joy: not a dream, not an image of the brain, not one of those shadowy chances imagination pictures . . . It was a godsend; and I inwardly thanked the God who had vouchsafed it. Outwardly I only thanked man, crying, 'Thank you, thank you, Monsieur!'

Monsieur curled his lip, gave me a vicious glance of the eye, and strode to his estrade. M. Paul was not at all a good little man, though he had good points.

Did I read my letter there and then? . . . I knew better. The cover with its address; the seal, with its three clear letters, was bounty and abundance for the present. I stole from the room, I procured the key of the great dormitory which was kept locked by day. I went to my bureau; with a sort of haste and trembling lest Madame should creep up-stairs and spy me, I opened a drawer, unlocked a box, and took out a case, and . . . folded the untasted treasure, yet all fair and inviolate, in silver paper, committed it to the case, shut up box and drawer, reclosed, relocked the dormitory, and returned to class, feeling as if fairy tales were true and fairy gifts no dream. Strange, sweet insanity! And this letter, the source of my joy, I had not yet read: did not yet know the number of its lines.

When I re-entered the schoolroom, behold M. Paul raging like a pestilence! Some pupil had not spoken audibly or distinctly enough to suit his ear and taste, and now she and others were weeping, and he was raving from his estrade almost livid. Curious to mention, as I appeared, he fell on me.

'Was I the mistress of these girls? Did I profess to teach them the conduct befitting ladies? – and did I permit and, he doubted not, encourage them to strangle their mother-tongue in their throats, to mince and mash it between their teeth, as if they had some base cause to be ashamed of the words they uttered? . . .'

What could I say to all this? Really nothing; and I hoped he would allow me to be silent. The storm recommenced.

'Every answer to his queries was then refused? It seemed to be considered . . . that the Professor of Literature was not worthy of a reply! These were new ideas; imported, he did not doubt, straight from "la Grande Bretaigne"; they savoured of island insolence and arrogance.'

Lull the second – the girls, not one of whom was ever known to weep a tear for the rebukes of any other master, now all melting like snow-statues before the intemperate heat of M. Emanuel: I, not yet much shaken, sitting down, and venturing to resume my work.

Something – either in my continued silence or in the movement of my hand, stitching – transported M. Emanuel beyond the last boundary of patience; he actually sprang from his estrade . . .

'Est-ce que vous avez l'intention de m'insulter?'[2] said he to me, in a low, furious voice . . .

It was time to soothe him a little if possible.

'Mais, Monsieur,' said I, 'I would not insult you for the world. I remember too well that you once said we should be friends.'

I did not intend my voice to falter, but it did: more, I think, through the agitation of late delight than in any spasm of present fear. Still there certainly was something in M. Paul's anger – a kind of passion of emotion – that specially tended to draw tears. I was not unhappy, nor much afraid, yet I wept.

'Allons, allons!'[3] said he presently, looking round and seeing the deluge universal. 'Decidedly I am a monster and a ruffian. I have only one pocket-handkerchief,' he added, 'but if I had twenty, I would offer you each one. Your teacher shall be your representative. Here, Miss Lucy.'

And he took forth and held out to me a clean silk handkerchief ... A very eloquent lesson he gave, and very kind and friendly was he to the close. Ere he had done, the clouds were dispersed and the sun shining out – tears were exchanged for smiles.

In quitting the room he paused once more at my desk.

'And your letter?' said he, this time not quite fiercely.

'I have not yet read it, Monsieur.'

'Ah! it is too good to read at once: you save it, as, when I was a boy, I used to save a peach whose bloom was very ripe?'

The guess came so near the truth, I could not prevent a suddenly-rising warmth in my face from revealing as much.

'You promise yourself a pleasant moment,' said he, 'in reading that letter; you will open it when alone – n'est-ce pas?[4] Ah! a smile answers. Well, well! one should not be too harsh; "la jeunesse n'a qu'un temps".'[5]

'Monsieur, Monsieur!' I cried or rather whispered after him, as he turned to go, 'do not leave me under a mistake. This is merely a friend's letter. Without reading it, I can vouch for that.'

'Je conçois, je conçois: on sait ce que c'est qu'un ami. Bonjour, Mademoiselle!'[6]

'But, Monsieur, here is your handkerchief.'

'Keep it, keep it, till the letter is read, then bring it me; I shall read the billet's tenor in your eyes.'

When he was gone, the pupils having already poured out of the school-room into the berceau, and thence into the garden and court to take their customary recreation before the five-o'clock dinner, I stood a moment thinking, and absently twisting the handkerchief round my arm. For some reason – gladdened, I think, by a sudden return of the golden glimmer of childhood, roused by an unwonted renewal of its buoyancy, made merry by the liberty of the closing hour, and, above all, solaced at heart by the joyous consciousness of that treasure in the case, box, drawer up-stairs, – I fell to playing with the handkerchief as if it were a ball, casting it into the air and catching it as it fell. The game was stopped by another hand than mine – a hand . . . stretched over my shoulder; it caught the extemporized plaything and bore it away with these sullen words:

'Je vois bien que vous vous moquez de moi et de mes effets.'[7]

Really that little man was dreadful: a mere sprite of caprice and ubiquity: one never knew either his whim or his whereabout.

A LOOK BACK AT THE HISTORY OF THE ISABELLE QUARTER

The Pensionnat dated from the early nineteenth century. Constructed in the French style, it was one of the more recent buildings in a street that had an interesting history. Rue d'Isabelle followed the line of the earliest (thirteenth-century) medieval city wall, although by the 1840s little remained visible of its ramparts and towers.

This street, so quiet yet so close to the royal palace, had been a much grander one in its day. It was created in the early seventeenth century by the Archduchess Isabella, daughter of Philip II of Spain and Governor of the Low Countries, to be used by the royal household when they went to services in the Collegiate Church of St Michael and St Gudule – later to become the Cathedral. When the construction of Rue Royale in the 1770s created a new route for that purpose, Rue d'Isabelle sank into obscurity and became a tranquil backwater. Even in the Brontës' day, visitors to the city would stumble on it only by chance, descending the steep steps from the Upper Town built in the late eighteenth century to the very different world of the Isabelle quarter on the hill sloping down to the oldest and lowest-lying part of the city, the Lower Town around Grand Place.

The cottage-like little houses lining Rue d'Isabelle were built by Isabella for the members of the prestigious guild, or company, of crossbowmen, the Grand Serment des Arbalétriers, to compensate them for the expropriation of part of their exercise

Gateway to the Jardin des Arbalétriers. This painting, dating from the
1890s, shows the gateway after it had been rebuilt, but it is similar to the
original one which the Brontës would often have passed when walking
along Rue d'Isabelle. Watercolour by Jacques Carabain (1890s)
Musée de la Ville de Bruxelles

ground for her street. What was left of this exercise ground or
Jardin des Arbalétriers was later occupied by the Pensionnat
garden. In the nineteenth century an old gateway to the garden
was still standing.

The Arbalétriers were important in the defence of the city and
Isabella was popular with them, particularly after demonstrating
her own skill with the crossbow when she won the Guild's annual
competition held on the sandy area (Sablon) next to the church
built by the Guild, Notre-Dame du Sablon. The winner always
became the next King of the Crossbowmen. Isabella succeeded
in shooting down the wooden bird placed as a target and was duly
crowned their Queen.

Charlotte must have learned something of the history of the
area and incorporated elements of it into *Villette*. Her tale of a nun
buried alive in punishment for some sin under a slab in the garden,
at the foot of the old pear tree, would have been suggested by a

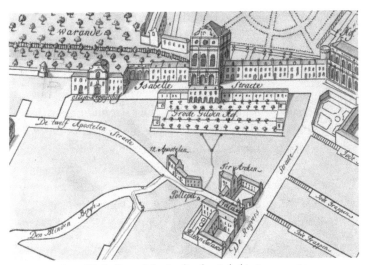

Rue d'Isabelle and the Jardin des Arbalétriers, c. 1750
Brussels City Archives

slab in the Pensionnat garden said to conceal the entrance to a secret subterranean passage through which the archers took flight when besieged; and to the fact that there had been convents and hospices near the site of the Pensionnat. It may also have been suggested by the story of Mme Heger's aunt, a nun who, forced to flee her convent in France during the French Revolution, had opened a school in Brussels,

The name Charlotte gives to Rue d'Isabelle in *Villette*, Rue Fossette, is likely to have been inspired by *Fossé-aux-Chiens* (dogs' ditch or channel), the old name for the area long before the street was built. The dogs in question were the hunting dogs of the Dukes of Brabant, the rulers of medieval Brussels who resided in the old Coudenberg Palace and had their kennels on the site. The ditch or channel probably referred to the channelling of one of the streams running down from the park to the river Senne below.

In the Brontës' time the steps leading down from General Belliard's statue were known as the 'Escalier de la Bibliothèque' or 'Passage de la Bibliothèque', after a mansion that had previously occupied the site. This 'Domus Isabellae', as it was called, was originally constructed by Isabella as a hall for the Master of the Grand Company of Crossbowmen, but in its latter days was used as a library to store books rescued from the old palace when it burned down in 1731. This hall was demolished in 1796 and the steps built soon afterwards on the place where it had stood.

All these layers of history and legend surrounding the site of the Pensionnat and its garden – the medieval convents, the crossbowmen's exercise ground, the story of their secret underground escape passage – must have contributed to the Gothic atmosphere of Charlotte's novel, what the British critic Gerald Cumberland, who visited the Pensionnat just before it was demolished, called 'the spirit of romance and mystery that suffuses each page of *Villette*'.[1]

Church of Notre Dame du Sablon. The Guild was granted land in the Sablon in return for its services defending the city and started to construct a church there in 1304. According to legend, a holy woman of Antwerp, Beatrice Soetkens, was instructed by the Virgin Mary to take an image of the Virgin to the Sablon. Beatrice put it in a boat which bore it up the Senne from Antwerp to Brussels. This image, known as 'Our Lady of the Little Boat', was placed in the church in 1346 and from then on carried by the crossbowmen in the annual procession, the Ommegang ('walk around') which first started in honour of this statue of the Virgin Mary. Originally a religious event, the Ommegang came to involve all the city's guilds and dignitaries and still takes place each summer, a colourful medieval pageant.

10

THE FATE OF THE ISABELLE QUARTER AND WHAT YOU CAN STILL SEE

The Pensionnat was demolished in 1909–10. By then, the whole of the area around it had already fallen victim to two massive redevelopment schemes. One of these was the construction of the Mont des Arts (the redevelopment of the museum quarter) on the slope between the Upper and Lower Towns and the other the planned Jonction Nord-Midi, the rail link between the North and South Stations, a project that was not to be completed for decades and included the construction of the Gare Centrale not far from the site of the Pensionnat. Leopold II's grandiose vision of a more modern and imposing Brussels had started the trend of insensitive development that has marred so much of the city ever since. It seems symbolic that his rule began with the covering over of the Senne – for reasons of sanitation – that deprived Brussels of its river and ended, in the year of his death in 1909, with the demolition of the last building left standing in the Isabelle quarter – the Hegers' school.

Leopold II (1835–1909), son of Leopold I, succeeded to the throne in 1865. He had big plans for Belgium, and his gargantuan urban development schemes, some of which were funded by his exploitation of the Congo, earned him the name of 'the Builder King'. In Brussels they included the Cinquantenaire complex (park, museums and triumphal arch), the Africa museum in Tervuren

81

The Hôtel Ravenstein today

and the massive Koekelberg Basilica that dominates the city's north-western skyline. His projects led to the destruction of many historical quarters.

Today our first impression is that nothing remains of the environs of the Pensionnat as they were in the Brontës' time. The site is buried for ever, much of it below the bulk of the Palais des Beaux-Arts or 'Bozar', built in the 1920s, between Rue Royale and Rue Ravenstein, one of the main streets in the new development.

But if we look hard we can still get one or two glimpses of the quarter the Brontës knew.

If we turn left out of Rue Baron Horta and walk along Rue Ravenstein we come to a splendid late-fifteenth-century aristo-cratic mansion (now greatly restored), the Hôtel Ravenstein or Cleves-Ravenstein, where, according to some accounts, Anne of Cleves was born. On their walks in the dark old streets near the Pensionnat – assuming that they felt safe enough in such streets to venture into them – Charlotte and Emily must surely have paused to gaze up at the turrets of this romantic building, a survivor of the

Rue Tèrarken in the nineteenth century, with the Hôtel Ravenstein
on the left
Brussels City Archives

Burgundian period. By its side are steps leading down to a little
street easily overlooked, at a much lower level than Rue Ravenstein,
which forms a bridge over it. If we go down the steps we find ourselves in a cobbled street, or what remains of it, a little stub of a

Above: Another view of the Rue St Laurent
Brussels City Archives

Opposite: The steps at the end of the old Rue Ravenstein, which
in the Brontës' time was called Rue St Laurent (it was renamed
in the 1850s). This was one of the narrow streets with 'Jewish steps'
linking Rue Terarken with Rue Montagne de la Cour. It disappeared
in the early twentieth century when the area was demolished and today's
Rue Ravenstein was built. Watercolour by Jacques Carabain (1890s)
Musée de la Ville de Bruxelles

street that for some reason was allowed to escape the developers'
pick-axes. Down here we are at the level of the old quarter, in the
truncated fragment of Rue Terarken, which joined up with Rue
d'Isabelle. Charlotte and Emily could have walked along it to
attend the Protestant chapel in Place du Musée.

Today it is a cul-de-sac, coming to an abrupt end at a goods
entrance to Bozar, its sole practical purpose to provide a passage
for delivery vans. Its other end passes under Rue Ravenstein to
an underground car park.

Rue Terarken ran parallel to Rue Montagne de la Cour and
was linked to it by several narrow streets, each of which led down
to Terarken by a series of steps known as the Escaliers des Juifs

('Jewish steps'). The name was a reminder that this was a Jewish quarter until the fourteenth century when the Jews were driven out, accused of stealing a Host from the Church of St Gudule and desecrating it. The steps by the Hôtel Ravenstein are the only ones that can be found today on the site of one of the original Escaliers des Juifs.

One of those narrow linking streets, Rue Villa Hermosa, partially escaped the pick-axes, and if you walk down it you can get the feel of the old cobbles under your feet. But it has lost its Jewish steps. They have long since vanished under the Bozar building, and today, like Terarken, the street is a cul-de-sac cut short by that building.

But there is one place left where you can actually still walk on Rue d'Isabelle itself. The street underwent an odd fate. In the late eighteenth century, long before Leopold II's projects, long even before the Brontës' arrival, the part of Rue d'Isabelle leading to the royal palace was buried underground when the ground was raised for the construction of Place Royale. This severed the street's links with the palace and put an end to its proud role as a route used by the royal family. The rest of it was to disappear completely or be buried under the redevelopments at the turn of the twentieth century. The stretch you can walk on today is the part that was buried in the eighteenth century and not a bit that the Brontës would have walked on. It is part of the archaeological site of the old Coudenberg Palace that has been excavated and opened to the public under the BELvue museum in Place Royale.

Rue Villa Hermosa and the popular Prince of Wales tavern.
Watercolour by Jacques Carabain (1890s)
Musée de la Ville de Bruxelles

Rue Royale and the entrance to the park – *Brussels City Archives*

AROUND PLACE ROYALE

In *Villette* Lucy compares Mme Beck's Pensionnat to a convent. Much of the action of the novel takes place within its walls. and the pervading atmosphere is somewhat claustrophobic. In real life, too, Charlotte and Emily, like any inmates of a boarding-school, spent much of their time closeted within the walls of the Pensionnat Heger, emerging only on Sundays and on Thursday afternoons, which were half-holidays. But all around them was a lively city. At the top of the Belliard steps, only a stone's throw away, was the Haute-Ville or Upper Town of the park and the palace, with its broad, well-lit streets and rattling carriages, while if you went in the other direction you descended the hill towards Grand Place and the older, grimmer, darker Basse-Ville with its gabled houses and medieval streets. The dramatic difference in levels can be appreciated if you look down the stairways and gardens of Mont des Arts, not far from the Belliard steps, towards the spire of the Hôtel de Ville in Grand Place. Much of the view down the Belliard steps themselves is today blocked by the Galerie Ravenstein, a 1950s shopping arcade whose once-elegant staircases descend towards the Lower Town.

Charlotte must have been well aware of the Pensionnat's position on the slope linking the two different Brussels, poised between two worlds. From descriptions in *Villette* we can infer that she sometimes explored the world below the school, the Lower Town where Lucy visits the sinister Mme Walravens, grandmother of the long-dead fiancée of Paul Emanuel, in whose house she learns the secrets of his life. The witch-like old woman lives in a

Place Royale and the Church of St Jacques sur Coudenberg
by Paul Lauters
Royal Library of Belgium

melancholy half-deserted square once inhabited by rich mer-
chants who have since moved on. Their once-grand houses are
dilapidated, and grass is growing between the flags. In some old
squares in Brussels today, the grass between the paving-stones
tells a similar story of neglect.

Other streets in the Basse-Ville were anything but half deserted.
They were teeming with the poorer *bruxellois*, crowded into tene-
ment buildings in squalid alleys. There were plenty of such streets
near the Pensionnat, and some of them would have been considered
to be unsafe, particularly for unaccompanied young ladies – and
not just after dark. The sisters usually headed upwards in the
direction of the Upper Town where most of their friends had
rented their accommodation.

Then, as now, the white mansion to the right as you ascended
the Belliard steps marked the transition to the Place Royale area.
This building acquired its present name, Hôtel Errera, from a
banker of Italian origin who resided there after the Brontës' time.
It is one of many neoclassical mansions in the Place Royale area,
which was developed when the charred ruins of the old ducal

Another view of Place Royale. In the centre is the tree of liberty planted by the French revolutionaries in 1794, which was replaced in 1848 by the statue of Godfrey of Bouillon that stands there today.
From Alphonse Wauters, Les Délices de la Belgique, *Société des Beaux Arts, Brussels, 1844*

The Royal Palace by H. Gérard, 1840
Royal Library of Belgium

Place du Musée in 1844. The Brontës came here every Sunday to worship
at the Protestant chapel, the 'Chapelle Royale'.
Brussels City Archives

Place du Musée today. The chapel, little changed since
the Brontës' time, is tucked away in the crescent-shaped
part of the building.
Photograph by Selina Busch

palace of Coudenberg ('cold hill') were finally demolished in the 1770s. Another such building is the Hôtel Bellevue. Today it is the BELvue museum, telling the story of Belgium since the revolution that led to its birth as an independent country; some of the fighting between the insurgents and the Dutch troops took place in the square and the park and on the Belliard steps. In the nineteenth century the Hôtel Bellevue was a popular base for English visitors, one of the most illustrious being Charlotte's hero the Duke of Wellington.

There were plenty of British residents in the area. Given Charlotte's frequent feelings of isolation in Brussels it is easy to forget by how many of her countrymen she was surrounded – but then it was her lot as a Brontë to feel constantly 'isolated in the midst of numbers'. The British population of Brussels had peaked following the Battle of Waterloo, when relatives of the wounded flocked over the Channel to care for them. Many stayed on when they found how much cheaper it was to live in Brussels than in England. By the 1840s their numbers had declined, but enough remained to form a thriving community. Then, as now, British expatriates had their amenities. Today they have shops such as the booksellers Waterstones; in the nineteenth century they had establishments such as the reading room with English journals run by a Mr Browne in Montagne de la Cour. They could even buy an English newspaper produced in the city.

A particularly distinguished English visitor was once glimpsed by Charlotte in Rue Royale. In her second summer in the city she saw a young countrywoman of around her own age ride by in a carriage. This was Queen Victoria, then aged twenty-three, on a visit to Belgium, with her uncle Leopold I, the first king of the newly independent country, and their respective consorts. The diminutive queen was chatting vivaciously and looked as carefree as Charlotte was depressed and lonely.

The church dominating Place Royale, St Jacques sur Coudenberg, was where the Hegers worshipped. In *Villette* it became 'St Jean Baptiste' whose bells Lucy can hear from the Pensionnat garden.

The Brontës, of course, did not worship at the Catholic St Jacques. They attended services at the Protestant chapel, the Chapelle Royale in the Place du Musée where the Rev. Jenkins officiated. He was not only the British Chaplain but Chaplain to the Protestant King Leopold.

The eighteenth-century white and gilt chapel nestles unobtrusively in one of the cream-coloured buildings of the palace built by Charles of Lorraine, a governor of the Austrian Netherlands, whose statue stands near by. The Place du Musée was formerly the courtyard of the eighteenth-century palace, now occupied by the royal art museums and the Royal Library. The chapel is virtually unchanged since the Brontës' time. It has been used for Protestant worship since Napoleon emancipated the Protestants during the period of French rule.

In *The Professor* William Crimsworth, searching for the girl with whom he has fallen in love, his erstwhile pupil Frances Evans Henri, a half-English Protestant, goes to the chapel hoping to see her there. Charlotte, often so critical of the people of her host country, was not wholly uncritical of her own countrymen; Crimsworth in *The Professor* notes how badly dressed the English churchgoers are compared with the elegant *bruxellois*. Unlike Emily, Charlotte had an eye for fashion, and her own dress sense was improved by her continental sojourn. She noticed that unlike English-made clothes the simple but pretty dresses run up by French dressmakers always seemed to fit perfectly.

The two English girls also sampled some of the culture on offer. In *Villette* Charlotte describes some pictures she saw at the 1842 Triennial Art Exhibition (*Salon*), held at the Musée des Beaux-Arts in the Charles de Lorraine Palace. M. Paul recommends a set of paintings called *The Life of a Woman* to Lucy, who rejects their view of a woman's destiny as a progression from pious bride to devoted mother and, finally, devout widow. Curiously, the painter was a woman, Fanny Geefs. Lucy is equally scathing about a very different picture, *Cleopatra*, depicting a voluptuous, scantily clad Egyptian dancing girl, which M. Paul considers unsuitable viewing for her. This has been identified as Edouard de Biefve's *Une Almée*.

Salle de la Grande Harmonie. This hall, built in the former courtyard
of the Hôtel d'Angleterre, was the scene of many a gala evening for the
bourgeoisie of Brussels. Berlioz conducted his fourth symphony there
on 26 September 1842. Emily was a keen musician, and, although we
know for certain only that Charlotte attended a concert in this hall
on 10 December 1843, the sisters may have gone to others of which they
left no record. This 1856 lithograph shows the room being used to host
a ball of the kind Lucy can hear carriages going to as she sits alone in
her 'shadow-world' at the Pensionnat.
G. *Renoy*, Bruxelles sous Léopold 1er: 25 ans de cartes porcelaine 1840–1865.
Crédit communal de Belgique, 1979

Charlotte took a keen interest in art – all the Brontë siblings
were competent amateur artists – and presumably saw other
paintings in Brussels that were more to her taste than these. The
city's art galleries had been one of the cultural treats she had looked
forward to most eagerly. The sisters would also have gone to occasional concerts. A concert Charlotte went to and describes in
Chapter 20 of *Villette* was attended by King Leopold and his Queen,
Louise-Marie (from her observation of him she believed the King
to be a fellow-sufferer of the depression that dogged both her and

The park and the Palais de la Nation (parliament building)
by Henri Borremans
Royal Library of Belgium

Lucy Snowe). The venue was the splendid new Salle de la Grande Harmonie – no longer standing – at the top of Rue de la Madeleine on the site of today's Place de l'Albertine. Charlotte, who was unused to such outings, was dazzled by the splendid white-and-gold interior of this concert hall with its huge chandelier 'like the work of eastern genii'.

They would also have heard music in the park during festivities such as those to mark the Feast of the Assumption or the 1830 Revolution. The bandstand where Lucy hears music at a festival to celebrate the anniversary of the revolution is still standing today. This scene from *Villette*, where Lucy wanders heartbroken and alone one summer night among the crowds in the illuminated park, appears in Chapter 15. Next, however, we are going to descend from the Upper Town and read about one of her forays into the sombre streets of the Basse-Ville.

Opposite: Leopold I. Before becoming King of the Belgians, Leopold of Saxe-Coburg (1790–1865) had been married to Princess Charlotte, the daughter of the British Prince Regent, the future George IV. It was a short-lived union; just eighteen months after their marriage in 1816 she died in childbirth. Another association with the British Royal Family was that he was the maternal uncle of Queen Victoria. Leopold was invited to become King of the newly formed Belgium in 1830. His investiture took place in 1831 on 21 July, which became the Belgian national holiday. In 1832 he married Louise-Marie d'Orléans, daughter of King Louis-Philippe of France. Leopold was a keen promoter of industrial development and rail construction, and the early years of his reign saw the opening in Belgium of the first railway line in continental Europe.
Portrait by Franz Xaver Winterhalter

I STOOD ABOUT THREE YARDS FROM A TALL,
SABLE-ROBED, SNOWY-VEILED WOMAN

Edmund Dulac, illustration for Villette, Dent, London, 1922

12

EXTRACT FROM VILLETTE (II)

A Burial: Lucy Buries Graham's Letters

Abridged from Chapter 26 of Villette

*Realizing that Graham ('Dr John') is not for her and that
she must renounce any hope of his returning her feelings, Lucy buries
his letters at the bottom of 'Methusaleh', the old pear-tree in the
Pensionnat garden, and faces the prospect that her life will continue
to be a solitary struggle. She wonders whether it is time to leave the
Pensionnat and move on.*

It was a fine frosty afternoon. The winter sun, already setting,
gleamed pale on the tops of the garden-shrubs in the 'allée
défendue'. One great old pear-tree – the nun's pear-tree – stood
up a tall dryad skeleton, grey, gaunt, and stripped. A thought struck
me – one of those queer fantastic thoughts that will sometimes
strike solitary people. I put on my bonnet, cloak and furs, and went
out into the city.

Bending my steps to the old historical quarter of the town, whose
hoar and overshadowed precincts I always sought by instinct in
melancholy moods, I wandered on from street to street, till, having
crossed a half-deserted 'place' or square, I found myself before a
sort of broker's shop; an ancient place, full of ancient things.

What I wanted was a metal box which might be soldered, or
a thick glass jar or bottle which might be stopped and sealed

hermetically. Amongst miscellaneous heaps, I found and purchased the latter article.

I then made a little roll of my letters, wrapped them in oiled silk, bound them with twine, and, having put them in the bottle, got the old Jew broker to stopper, seal, and make it air-tight. While obeying my directions, he glanced at me now and then, suspiciously, from under his frost-white eye lashes. I believe he thought there was some evil deed on hand. In all this I had a dreary something – not pleasure – but a sad, lonely satisfaction. The impulse under which I acted, the mood controlling me, were similar to the impulse and the mood which had induced me to visit the confessional. With quick walking I regained the pensionnat just at dark, and in time for dinner.

At seven o'clock the moon rose. At half-past seven, when the pupils and teachers were at study . . . I shawled myself, and, taking the sealed jar, stole out through the first-classe door, into the berceau and thence into the 'allée défendue'.

Methusaleh, the pear-tree, stood at the further end of this walk, near my seat: he rose up, dim and grey, above the lower shrubs round him. Now Methusaleh, though so very old, was of sound timber still; only there was a hole, or rather a deep hollow, near his root. I knew there was such a hollow, hidden partly by ivy and creepers growing thick round; and there I meditated hiding my treasure. But I was not only going to hide a treasure – I meant also to bury a grief. That grief over which I had lately been weeping, as I wrapped it in its winding-sheet, must be interred.

Well, I cleared away the ivy, and found the hole; it was large enough to receive the jar, and I thrust it deep in. In a tool shed at the bottom of the garden, lay the relics of building-materials, left by masons lately employed to repair a part of the premises. I fetched thence a slate and some mortar, put the slate on the hollow, secured it with cement, covered the whole with black mould, and, finally, replaced the ivy. This done, I rested, leaning against the tree; lingering, like any other mourner, beside a newly-sodded grave.

The air of the night was very still, but dim with a peculiar mist, which changed the moonlight into a luminous haze. In this air, or this mist, there was some quality – electrical, perhaps – which acted in strange sort upon me. I felt then as I had felt a year ago in England – on a night when the aurora borealis was streaming and sweeping round heaven, when, belated in lonely fields, I had paused to watch that mustering of an army with banners – that quivering of serried lances – that swift ascent of messengers from below the north star to the dark, high keystone of heaven's arch. I felt, not happy, far otherwise, but strong with reinforced strength.

If life be a war, it seemed my destiny to conduct it single-handed. I pondered now how to break up my winter-quarters – to leave an encampment where food and forage failed. Perhaps, to effect this change, another pitched battle must be fought with fortune; if so, I had a mind to the encounter: too poor to lose, God might destine me to gain. But what road was open? – what plan available?

On this question I was still pausing, when the moon, so dim hitherto, seemed to shine out somewhat brighter: a ray gleamed even white before me, and a shadow became distinct and marked. I looked more narrowly, to make out the cause of this well-defined contrast appearing a little suddenly in the obscure alley: whiter and blacker it grew on my eye: it took shape with instantaneous transformation. I stood about three yards from a tall, sable-robed, snowy-veiled woman.

Five minutes passed. I neither fled nor shrieked. She was there still. I spoke.

'Who are you? and why do you come to me?'

She stood mute. She had no face – no features: all below her brow was masked with a white cloth; but she had eyes, and they viewed me.

I felt, if not brave, yet a little desperate; and desperation will often suffice to fill the post and do the work of courage. I advanced one step. I stretched out my hand, for I meant to touch her. She seemed to recede. I drew nearer: her recession, still silent, became swift. A mass of shrubs, full-leaved evergreens, laurel and dense yew, intervened between me and what I followed. Having passed that obstacle, I looked and saw nothing. I waited. I said, – 'If you have any errand to me, come back and deliver it.' Nothing spoke or re-appeared.

This time there was no Dr. John to whom to have recourse: there was no one to whom I dared whisper the words, 'I have again seen the nun.'

13

THE BRONTËS' FRIENDS
IN BRUSSELS

In *Villette* Lucy's solitude is relieved by the exhibitions, plays and concerts to which she is taken by Graham Bretton and his mother, who show her glimpses of life in the bright lights of the Haute-Ville and rescue her temporarily from the depression to which, like her creator, she is so prone.

In real life, Charlotte and Emily – mainly Charlotte, as Emily made little effort to forge relationships outside her own family – had several English friends in the city.

The Jenkins Family in Chaussée d'Ixelles

There were of course Evan Jenkins, the British Chaplain, and his wife, who had recommended the Pensionnat. Mrs Jenkins extended an open invitation to the two girls to join the Jenkins family for lunch on Sundays. As the house was some way out of the centre, two of their sons had the job of escorting the girls there.

The Jenkins family lived in Chaussée d'Ixelles. It is now a teeming shopping street, but in their time it led through the faubourg (suburb) of Namur beyond the Porte de Namur to the village of Ixelles. The house where the family lived is no longer standing, but it probably stood at approximately the location of the present number 144.

The two Jenkins sons became chaplains in Brussels like their father. Perhaps, in later years, they would entertain British residents of the city with tales of those excruciating Sunday lunches with the Brontë sisters. They had no small talk. Emily never bothered to converse with people who did not interest her. Charlotte was slightly more sociable but painfully shy. In the Jenkinses' house Emily never opened her mouth, while Charlotte did sometimes become animated in conversation but had a habit of wheeling gradually round on her chair, away from the person she was speaking to, until her face was hidden from them. The boys complained, too, about the torture of trying to make conversation on the walk to the house, and in the end the Sunday lunch arrangement so kindly made was dropped.

On his death in 1849, only a few years after the sisters left Brussels, Rev. Jenkins was buried in the Protestant cemetery described in *The Professor,* beyond the Porte de Louvain. Crimsworth, trying to trace Frances Henri, finds her in this cemetery visiting her aunt's grave. It was a picturesque spot, with willows and cypresses, and contained the tombs of some of the British soldiers killed at Waterloo. But in the 1870s this graveyard was closed when houses were built on the land where it lay. Evan Jenkins's grave, along with many others, was transferred to the big new city cemetery in the outlying district of Evere, where you can still see it today. Beside his tomb lies that of one of the sons who used to have to escort a silent Charlotte and Emily Brontë to Sunday lunch in the Chaussée d'Ixelles.

Mary and Martha Taylor at Koekelberg

The sisters were much more talkative with the best friends they had in Brussels, Mary and Martha Taylor. In *Shirley,* her novel of industrial unrest in Yorkshire, Charlotte was later to immortalize them as Rose and Jessy Yorke, the daughters of a mill-owner. Mary Taylor, who had first put the idea of studying in Brussels into Charlotte's head, was an old school friend. Down-to-earth, outspoken, open-minded and a feminist, she would often try to urge Charlotte out of depression and inertia and into action, advising

The Château de Koekelberg boarding-school
where Mary and Martha Taylor studied in
1841-2. Painting by Henri Pauwels dated 1887
Reproduced in Joan Stevens, Mary Taylor, Friend
of Charlotte Brontë: Letters from New Zealand
and Elsewhere.
Oxford University Press, Oxford 1972

her to leave Brussels when she became obsessed with M. Heger.
Mary never married and later lived for a period in New Zealand,
where she opened a shop. Her younger sister Martha, talkative and
funny, charmed everyone she met. Jessy Yorke in *Shirley* is 'gay and
chattering, arch, original . . . with her little piquant face, engaging
prattle, and winning ways . . . much loved . . . much loving'.[1]

The two sisters were studying German and French at the
Château de Koekelberg boarding-school in the north-west of the
city beyond the Porte de Flandre. The directress, Mme Goussaert
(née Phelps), was an Englishwoman married to a Belgian.

The Porte de Flandre in the north of the city by Henri Borremans. The
Brontës would have entered through this city gate when they arrived in
Brussels by stagecoach from Ostend in 1842 and passed through it on their
way to the Taylors' school in the suburb of Koekelberg.
Royal Library of Belgium

The school vanished long ago. It was demolished in the
1880s, and the area has today changed beyond recognition. There
is a metro station now in Place Simonis close to the site of the Taylors' school. Pictures of the building show a large square mansion;
it was surrounded by trees and approached up an avenue. In Charlotte and Emily's time a faubourg had already grown up outside the
Porte de Flandre, but the area round the school was still countrified
and when the Brontë girls went out to Koekelberg towards the end
of March 1842 to spend a day with the Taylor girls they would have
seen plenty of tree-lined avenues leading to big houses.

We have a vivid record of that day, because Charlotte, Mary
and Martha wrote a joint letter to their friend Ellen Nussey who
had been at school with them.

It was to stand out as a happy day for Charlotte, already feeling homesick. Clearly the two Taylor sisters, who wrote most of
the letter, did not share her tendency to depression. They bubble

over with high spirits. Like Charlotte they laugh at the oddities of the other inmates of their school but do so in a spirit of fun, very different from the sourness of her own reflections on her schoolfellows and teachers.

The Château de Koekelberg school resembled the Brussels of today in being a mix of nationalities and a cacophony of languages. Teachers and girls were a mixture of Belgian, English, French and German. Attempting to learn French and German, and surrounded by people speaking languages not their own with amusing results as idiomatic expressions were rendered literally in other tongues, Martha complained that 'in attempting to acquire other languages I have almost forgotten the little I knew of my own'.[2]

Mary and Martha's brother Joseph, who with Mary had accompanied the Brontës to Brussels, was a wool merchant who often travelled between Yorkshire and Belgium on business and sometimes acted as postman for the girls between the two. The letter written that day was to be delivered by him to Ellen. 'When you see my brother Joe have the kindness to pull his hair right well for me,' Martha playfully instructs her.

Apart from her reincarnation as Jessy Yorke in *Shirley*, Martha flashes into life whenever we glimpse her in letters. But just over six months later she was dead of cholera.

She was buried among the willows of the Protestant cemetery. On long solitary walks in her second year in Brussels, without Emily, when many of her English friends had left the city and she was becoming more and more depressed at the Pensionnat, Charlotte would visit Martha's grave. She was to write of it in *Shirley*:

> Do you know this place? No, you never saw it; but you recognize the nature of these trees, this foliage, – the cypress, the willow, the yew. Stone crosses like these are not un-familiar to you, nor are these dim garlands of everlasting flowers. Here is the place; green sod and a gray marble head-stone – Jessy sleeps below. She lived through an April day; much loved was she, much loving. She often, in her brief life,

shed tears, she had frequent sorrows; she smiled between, gladdening whatever saw her. Her death was tranquil and happy in Rose's guardian arms, for Rose had been her stay and defence through many trials: the dying and the watching English girls were at that hour alone in a foreign country, and the soil of that country gave Jessy a grave. (*Shirley*, Chapter 9)

Martha was thus destined to stay on in Brussels for ever after the Brontës and her sister (who soon left to take up a teaching post in Germany) had departed it never to return. But she was not allowed to sleep on undisturbed in the Protestant cemetery. All the graves were removed when it was closed. Over the years attempts have been made to find Martha's new burial place. Was her grave among those transferred to the new burial ground in Evere? Brontë enthusiasts have hunted for it, but it has never been found. When the old cemetery closed, notices appeared in British newspapers

An artist's impression of the Protestant cemetery, used by Charlotte as the setting for William Crimsworth's and Frances Henri's reunion in *The Professor*
E.M. Wimperis, illustration for The Professor, *Smith, Elder and Co., London, 1873*

informing the relatives of those interred there how to obtain rights to plots in the new one. Mary Taylor was still alive and was back in England, but even assuming she saw these notices, it is highly unlikely she would have paid for a new grave for her sister; the Protestant Chapel's records show that at the time of Martha's death the Taylor family paid only for a 'second-class' funeral and did not buy a burial plot in perpetuity.

Martha's name is not listed in the records of the Evere cemetery. This is probably because her remains were taken to a mass grave on its eastern edge.

The site of the former Protestant cemetery still has a certain charm today although it is now surrounded by houses. A grass plot in front of an apartment building marks its approximate location. A walk today along Chaussée de Louvain, following the route Charlotte and Emily would have taken, gives no idea of the country road they knew; it is a busy traffic thoroughfare and shopping street. But as soon as you turn off it down Rue du Noyer you find yourself in a tranquil spot. You can stand on the grass in an open space surrounded by Brussels town houses and try to picture the melancholy but romantic scene immortalized in *The Professor* and *Shirley*.

The Wheelwrights in Rue Royale

The Brontës knew a couple of interesting English families in Brussels. Such families came to the city in search of educational opportunities for their children – a spell at a foreign school was considered beneficial – and in some cases business openings for themselves. Another common reason for moving abroad was money difficulties; creditors did not follow you across the Channel, and school fees and the cost of living were much lower in Brussels than in Britain. Dr Thomas Wheelwright, a London physician, moved his large family there because of financial problems, probably caused by his failing eyesight. His five daughters were pupils at the Pensionnat. The family arrived in Brussels in July 1842. For the first couple of months, while their parents travelled in Germany, the girls were left at the Pensionnat together with the Brontës and the few other boarders who did not go home for the vacation. These summer months at the Pensionnat in the company of Emily and the Wheelwright girls were much more pleasant for Charlotte than the vacation of 1843 when she was practically the only person who stayed on at the school.

The Wheelwrights rented an apartment in the Hôtel Cluysenaar towards the north end of Rue Royale. This building subsequently underwent various transformations and bore little resemblance to the one on the site today, the Hôtel Astoria, dating from the early twentieth century, which in its heyday was the grandest hotel in town and hosted many foreign celebrities.

The Hôtel Cluysenaar was built in 1838 by the rising young Dutch architect Cluysenaar, whose most famous creation, dating from a few years after the Brontës' departure, is the Galeries Saint-Hubert, the elegant shopping arcade. The Cluysenaar apartment building was in a fashionable part of town near the site of the future Gare du Nord.

Connected to this building by a covered passageway was Rue Notre Dame aux Neiges in an older and much less smart area. Frances Henri lodges in a street of that name in *The Professor*. Charlotte probably saw the street on visits to the Wheelwrights. Frances earns a living as a lace-mender and the area round Rue Notre Dame aux Neiges was traditionally one of lace-makers, who, it was said, used to pray in the chapel that gave the street its name, Our Lady of the Snows, for their lace to be as white as snow. But by the Brontës' time the reputation of the area was becoming rather less immaculate. In the 1870s it was demolished – always the preferred solution of Brussels city planners – on the grounds that it was an insalubrious area rife with prostitution. Today's Rue de l'Enseignement is on the approximate site of the street whose name Charlotte, no doubt ignorant of its reputation, uses for the one where Crimsworth visits and woos Frances in her tiny lodgings.

The Cluysenaar apartment building, with its wide staircases which the little Wheelwright girls amused themselves running up

The Wheelwrights' apartment was in the Hôtel
Cluysenaar on Rue Royale, probably the model
for the Hotel Crécy in *Villette*.
Reproduced in Jacques Dubreucq, Bruxelles 1000: Une
histoire capitale, *published by the author, Brussels, 1999*

In the early twentieth century the Hôtel Cluysenaar was rebuilt
as the smart Hôtel Astoria.
Photograph in Hôtel Astoria brochure, c. 1911

and down, is thought to have inspired the Hôtel Crécy in *Villette* where the Count De Bassompierre and his daughter Paulina, who wins the heart of Graham Bretton, have their apartment. In Chapter 23 of *Villette* Charlotte describes the Hôtel Crécy as 'an hotel in the foreign sense: a collection of dwelling-houses, not an inn – a vast, lofty pile, with a huge arch to its street-door, leading through a vaulted covered way, into a square all built round'.

At parties at the De Bassompierres' Lucy has some of her rare tastes of life in high society in *Villette*. Had Charlotte herself been invited to such parties it is unlikely that she would have felt comfortable at them; in later life, when she was a famous author being fêted on visits to London, she suffered agonies of shyness at large gatherings. But her social skills were not put to the test in this way in Brussels, and she enjoyed her visits to the Wheelwrights. Like the Taylors they were a lively and stimulating family. Theirs was one of the few households where she felt relaxed, just as she always did when she stayed with the Taylors in Yorkshire. She remained friendly with Laetitia, the eldest of the daughters, for the rest of her life. The Wheelwrights were fond of her in return, although their liking did not extend to Emily; the three youngest Wheelwright girls were among the pupils with whom Emily made herself unpopular by giving them piano lessons during their recreation periods.

Tragedy struck this family, too, in Brussels when the youngest of Emily's reluctant little piano pupils, Julia, died of typhus only two months after Martha Taylor and was buried near her in the Protestant cemetery. She was seven years old. The funeral records of the Protestant Chapel show that she had only a 'third-class' funeral, which meant that unlike Martha she didn't get a headstone. Her remains doubtless ended up with Martha's in a mass grave in Evere when the old cemetery was closed.

The Dixons in Rue de la Régence

Finally, there was the Dixon family at 11 Rue de la Régence. This house is no longer standing; the street numbering has changed and today's number 11 is in a part of Rue de la Régence that was not yet built in the Brontës' time. The building where the Dixons lodged probably disappeared when the art museums were expanded.

Charlotte knew them through their family connection with the Taylors; Abraham Dixon was an uncle of Mary and Martha's. He was a man of ideas and projects, a not always successful inventor who was trying to sell his patents to the Belgian woollen manufacturing industry. A widower, he was living in Brussels with various family members including his daughter Mary with whom Charlotte struck up a friendship at the start of her second year. A son of his who worked for a firm in Birmingham travelled between England and Belgium on business and carried Charlotte's letters for her just as Mary Taylor's brother did.

Despite Charlotte's frequent complaints of loneliness in Brussels she was fortunate in having several congenial friends there, one of whom was Mary Dixon. In later years she stayed in touch with her, as she did with Laetitia Wheelwright. But like her other English friends in Brussels, the Dixons did not stay long, and when Mary left for Germany in the summer of 1843 she was one of the people Charlotte missed most. It is still a common experience in Brussels today: you make friends, fellow expatriates, bond quickly in a foreign country but then lose these new acquaintances when they move back to their home countries or on to a new posting abroad.

Where Was 'La Terrasse'?

In *Villette* the place described most evocatively, apart from the Pensionnat itself, is 'La Terrasse', the 'little château' or manor house on the outskirts of Brussels where Graham Bretton lives with his mother and where he takes Lucy to recuperate when she has a kind of nervous breakdown.

Charlotte Brontë always put her own experience into her novels. If she visited a friend's home there was a good chance that it would appear as that of a character in one of her books, and it is possible that La Terrasse was inspired by a real house she saw. But which one? The Taylors' Château de Koekelberg school in the north of the city, perhaps, at the end of its avenue of trees? Or was it more likely to have been inspired by a building seen in the south of Brussels? Lucy refers to it as being down an avenue leading off a *chaussée* a mile beyond the 'Porte de Crécy'. There was no gate of that name in Brussels, but since Crécy was a battle in which the English were victorious, could it be a veiled reference to Waterloo? Was La Terrasse perhaps one of the large houses off the Chaussée de Waterloo? Possibly it was an amalgam of more than one little château spotted by Charlotte.

No such doubt surrounds the origin of Graham and Mrs Bretton, although unlike most of the other characters in *Villette* they are not based on people Charlotte met in Brussels. Graham was modelled on her publisher George Smith, who snapped up *Jane Eyre* and published it within a few weeks of receiving it. She quickly became friendly with the handsome, charming Smith and used to stay with him and his mother ('Mrs Bretton') on trips to London. Lucy's impressions of the interior of La Terrasse may owe something to the Smiths' London residence. But in its outer appearance, the Brettons' château seems to be typical of the old-fashioned manor houses to be seen in and around the Belgian capital.

14

BRUSSELS IN THE
BRONTËS' TIME

Brussels is a beautiful city. (Letter to Ellen Nussey, May 1842)

I have tramped about a great deal and tried to get a clearer acquaintance with the streets of Bruxelles . . . I go out and traverse [them] sometimes for hours together. (Letter from Charlotte Brontë to Emily, 2 September 1843)

I had crossed the Place Royale, and got into the Rue Royale, thence I had diverged into the Rue de Louvain – an old and quiet street. I remember that, feeling a little hungry, and not desiring to go back and take my share of the 'gouter,' now on the refectory-table at Pelet's – to wit, pistolets and water – I stepped into a baker's and refreshed myself on a couc (?) – it is a Flemish word, I don't know how to spell it – à corinthe-anglice, a currant bun – and a cup of coffee; and then I strolled on towards the Porte de Louvain. Very soon I was out of the city, and slowly mounting the hill, which ascends from the gate. (*The Professor*, Chapter 19)

In 1842 the population of Brussels was not much more than 100,000, and in places the countryside was still close to the boulevards ringing the city (today's inner ring road) on the site of the former defensive walls. Charlotte and Emily's walk to the Protestant cemetery, only about a kilometre from the Porte de Louvain, took them along a country road.

However, Brussels was already beginning to spread apace beyond these boulevards, which followed the line of the 'pentagon', the five-sided or heart-like shape of the old town. New faubourgs had sprung up outside the gates – Faubourg de Namur beyond the Porte de Namur on the way to the house of the Jenkins family in Ixelles, Faubourg de Flandre outside the Porte de Flandre on the way to the Koekelberg school. The neat little house M. Paul rents for Lucy, where she is to open a school while she waits for him to return from the West Indies, is in a suburb to which Charlotte gives the imaginary name of Faubourg Clotilde.

It was a time of expansion and development for Belgium generally, which since gaining its independence had become a confident, liberal and rapidly modernizing country. Like Britain, the country was in the midst of an industrial revolution, the first in continental Europe. It was also the first country on the Continent to build a railway, with the opening of a service between Brussels and Mechelen in 1835. In the early years of the railway, trains arrived in Brussels at a station by the Canal de Willebroeck called Allée Verte, beside the popular avenue of that name. But by the beginning of the 1840s there was already a Gare du Midi in the south of the city and work had started on the Gare du Nord, just off the Boulevard du Jardin Botanique, which was to replace Allée Verte. When Charlotte returned alone to Brussels in 1843 she travelled by train there from Ostend, a six-hour journey. Making the journey by stagecoach, as the two girls and their father did in 1842, was already becoming outmoded.

As a small capital Brussels could not of course compete with Paris or London in brilliance and variety; some travellers found it rather dull and Thackeray, visiting at the time the Brontës were there, mocked the small scale of everything, the city's 'absurd kind of Lilliput look'.[1] But other visitors and contemporary guide books paint a picture of a city of spacious, elegant squares full of shops

The first railway station in Brussels, Allée Verte, opened in 1835
From Louis Hymans, Bruxelles à travers les ages, *Bruylandt-Christophe et Cie,
Brussels, 1884, Vol. III; Brussels City Archives*

and cafés, the liveliest after Place Royale being Place de la Monnaie
with its Royal Theatre. Grand hotels possessed every amenity as
well as supplying improbably abundant meals; Thackeray was
astounded by the twenty dishes his own hotel offered for dinner.

Smart shopping streets such as Rue de la Madeleine were
packed with luxury establishments for the well-to-do. This street
has since been truncated and is now a shadow of its former self
but even today retains a few elegant shops.

Contemporary images show an animated and cheerful
town. One of its great attractions was the park. There were plays

Rue de la Madeleine was one of the smartest shopping streets.
This engraving dates from 1825.
Brussels City Archives

Boulevard du Jardin Botanique and the botanical gardens
by W.H. Bartlett, *c.* 1840
Royal Library of Belgium

at the Théâtre du Parc, entertainment at the 'Vauxhall', another park theatre, and, on fine days, music at the bandstand; the paths teemed with carriages and strollers.

The boulevards were another of the city's charms. In letters home Charlotte describes 'tramping' about Brussels for hours, particularly when depressed, and specifically mentions tramping along the boulevards. This was before the time of those built in the later nineteenth century by Leopold II – Boulevard Anspach, for example, created on top of the Senne when the river was covered over. Charlotte was referring to the pleasant tree-lined roads encircling the city that had been created under the period of Napoleonic rule in the early years of the century on the site of the fourteenth-century city walls when these were demolished.

In her time the boulevards were still dotted with toll gates manned by guards, for the unpopular toll levied on many goods entering the city was not abolished until 1860. Lucy Snowe, who has set out from La Terrasse for a night out with her friends the Brettons, describes entering Brussels by carriage in the days of the toll gates:

The Porte de Louvain by Paul Lauters. The Brontës would
have walked through this city gate on their way to the Protestant
cemetery to visit the grave of Martha Taylor.
Royal Library of Belgium

The snug comfort of the close carriage on a cold though
fine night, the pleasure of setting out with companions so
cheerful and friendly, the sight of the stars glinting fitfully
through the trees as we rolled along the avenue; then the
freer burst of the night-sky when we issued forth to the
open chaussée, the passage through the city gates, the
lights there burning, the guards there posted, the pretence
of inspection to which we there submitted, and which
amused us so much – all these small matters had for me,
in their novelty, a peculiar exhilarating charm. (*Villette*,
Chapter 20)

The fortress-like gates of earlier times had gone by then,
with the exception of the Porte de Hal in the south, still in place
today but much embellished. The gates Charlotte and Emily
passed through were of much newer construction. The toll booths
at the Porte de Namur between which they would have walked on

The Porte de Hal, by the Brontës' time the only surviving medieval
city gateway, as depicted by Paul Lauters. It is still in place
today, much restored.
Brussels City Archives

their way to the Jenkins' house can still be seen, although not in
their original location because they were reconstructed by the
entrance of the Bois de la Cambre at the end of Avenue Louise.

The boulevards offered an eight-kilometre round walk,
with views over the countryside. Today one can still walk along
Boulevard de Waterloo or Boulevard du Régent, but as the traffic
thunders by it is difficult to conjure up in imagination the elegance
of the spacious avenues where Charlotte and Emily sometimes
took their exercise. Boulevard du Jardin Botanique, for example,
took them past the impressive botanical gardens, which like the
Park have today lost something of their former splendour.

One of the most popular walks for the *bruxellois* was to follow the Allée Verte, the tree-lined avenue that led along the Canal
de Willebroeck to the royal family's palace in Laeken. Used by the
faithful in the time of the Archduchess Isabella as a route of
pilgrimage to the church of Notre Dame de Laeken, it had

One of the toll booths (customs houses) of the Porte de Namur,
the gate the Brontës would have passed through on their way
to Sunday lunch with Rev. Jenkins and his family in Chaussée
d'Ixelles. The booths have been reconstructed at the entrance
to the Bois de la Cambre.

since become a fashionable promenade. In a school composition
written in German Charlotte described going for a picnic in the
countryside with another teacher and some of the pupils, returning to the city along the Allée Verte.[2]

Shaded by four rows of venerable lime trees, this wide avenue
was the place to head to on a Sunday to show off your carriage,
your horses, your *toilette* and your *cachemire*. (Mrs Sweeny, the
whisky-tippling nursemaid of dubious origin employed to look
after Mme Beck's children until ousted by Lucy, maintains her
standing in the establishment largely thanks to her possession of
a cashmere shawl.)

Its starting-point was near the location of today's Yser
metro station, and although one can still stroll beside the canal
nothing remains today to remind one of the route's former glories
as depicted in old prints. Its popularity waned in the 1860s, when

The Allée Verte, Brussels' most fashionable promenade in the
Brontës' time, as depicted by F. Stroobant
Brussels City Archives

the fashionable started to desert it for the new Avenue Louise
leading to the Bois de la Cambre.

Most of these places were in the new, posh Upper Town
with the symmetrical French-style buildings that had transformed Brussels into a 'miniature Paris', as it was sometimes called.
By contrast, there was the old Basse-Ville of winding cobbled
streets, irregular Flemish-style houses with stepped gables and
old churches and convents. There were ornate Baroque churches
such as the seventeenth-century St Jean Baptiste, originally the
church of the Béguinage, an enclosed quarter for women who
belonged to the lay religious order of Béguines. Confusingly,
this was not the model for the church called St Jean Baptiste in
Villette, which clearly refers to St Jacques sur Coudenberg in Place
Royale. Equally confusingly, although a Béguinage church is
mentioned in *Villette* its description does not altogether fit the
one in Brussels. We are told that after Lucy emerges from her

The Church of St Jean Baptiste du Béguinage by F. Stroobant
Brussels City Archives

confession in an unnamed church, she falls down in a faint in front of another one, 'an old church belonging to a community of Béguines'. But this fictional church has a giant spire, which St Jean Baptiste au Béguinage does not. Lucy describes it as being in a part of the old town unfamiliar to her, 'full of narrow streets of picturesque, ancient, and mouldering houses'. Lucy Snowe's

Grand Place in 1843 by H. Gérard
Royal Library of Belgium

Béguinage church is doubtless an imaginary one fashioned out of Charlotte's memories of more than one church glimpsed in the Basse-Ville.

Later in the century many old streets were destroyed in the interests of what would today be called health and safety. Their insalubrious alleys were a breeding ground for disease such as the cholera that carried off thousands of inhabitants in the 1860s. But prints of the period convey the picturesqueness of the old town below the Pensionnat that so fascinated Charlotte.

She does not specifically mention Grand Place but must have seen it on occasional visits to the Old Town. At the end of February 1843 M. Heger took her and one of the pupils to see the carnival festivities that preceded Ash Wednesday, with their masks and disguises and processions along the streets near Grand Place. Charlotte dismissed the spectacle as 'mummery' but relished the animation of the crowds and would have stored the vivid impressions away as elements of the atmosphere of Catholic continental 'Villette'.

Manneken Pis
From Alphonse Wauters, Les Délices de Belgique, *Société des Beaux Arts, Brussels,
1844; Brussels City Archives*

Lucy Snowe's expeditions to the Basse-Ville are few and far between, but this makes her rare descriptions of its dark streets all the more powerful. That they fired her creator's imagination is clear from scenes such as the one we have read where Lucy goes into a bric-à-brac shop in the old quarter.

You can still walk in the old streets of Brussels today and peer into the dusty windows of such shops, crammed with the discarded contents of people's attics. A latter-day Lucy Snowe would be unlikely to bury the letters of a hopeless love at the bottom of her garden. But should she have such letters and be in want of an old bottle with a stopper and seal in which to inter them she would have no trouble finding one in a junk shop in a back street not dissimilar to the ones that drew Charlotte, in her solitary second year, out of the Rue d'Isabelle and into Brussels Old Town.

Next we are going to return to the Upper Town to read about a nocturnal visit Lucy pays to the Park. Having buried her feelings for Graham Bretton, she has gradually fallen in love with Paul Emanuel. But just as she starts to feel confident of his love her happiness is shattered by the news that he is leaving for the West

Indies. Once again she falls into a depression. Mme Beck, who has been doing everything possible to separate the two, has given her an opiate intended to make her sleep; instead, she becomes wakeful and leaves her bed to sneak into the fête, but perhaps because of the opiate everything around her is as hallucinatory as a strange dream. It is one of the most haunting passages in the novel.

A *Concert in the Park* by Jobard, *c.* 1830. This lithograph dates from ten years before the cast-iron bandstand (*kiosque à musique*) that had been erected by Charlotte's time and which she doubtless had in mind when writing this scene. This shows an earlier wooden kiosk.
Brussels City Archives

15

EXTRACT FROM VILLETTE (III)

Lucy Goes to the Park at Night

Abridged from Chapter 38 of Villette

*The scenes described, including the concert Lucy hears at the bandstand, were
based on fêtes in the park during Charlotte's stay. The 'Jager' or huntsmen's
chorus (German jäger or hunter) may have been inspired by music in the
park in the summer of 1843 – for example, Girschner's 'Jagd Chor'
at a concert on 15 August, Assumption Day, or a piece called 'Choeur des
montagnards', which was sung by a huge choir at a concert on 24 September
to mark the Revolution.*

Ah! the sedative had been administered. In fact, they had given me
a strong opiate. I was to be held quiet for one night.

The household came to bed, the night-light was lit, the
dormitory hushed. Sleep soon reigned . . .

I know not whether Madame had over-charged or under-
charged the dose; its result was not that she intended. Instead of
stupor, came excitement. I became alive to new thought – to reverie
peculiar in colouring. A gathering call ran among the faculties,
their bugles sang, their trumpets rang an untimely summons.
Imagination was roused from her rest, and she came forth impetu-
ous and venturous . . .

'Look forth and view the night!' was her cry; and when I
lifted the heavy blind from the casement close at hand – with her

own royal gesture, she showed me a moon supreme, in an element deep and splendid.

To my gasping senses she made the glimmering gloom, the narrow limits, the oppressive heat of the dormitory, intolerable. She lured me to leave this den and follow her forth into dew, coolness, and glory.

She brought upon me a strange vision of Villette at midnight. Especially she showed the park, the summer-park, with its long alleys all silent, lone and safe; among these lay a huge stone-basin – that basin I knew, and beside which I had often stood – deep-set in the tree-shadows, brimming with cool water, clear, with a green, leafy, rushy bed. What of all this? The park-gates were shut up, locked, sentinelled: the place could not be entered.

Could it not? A point worth considering; and while revolving it, I mechanically dressed. Utterly incapable of sleeping or lying still – excited from head to foot – what could I do better than dress?

The gates were locked, soldiers set before them: was there, then, no admission to the park?

The other day, in walking past, I had seen, without then attending to the circumstance, a gap in the paling – one stake broken down: I now saw this gap again in recollection – saw it very plainly . . . A man could not have made his way through that aperture . . . but I thought I might: I fancied I should like to try, and once within, at this hour the whole park would be mine – the moonlight, midnight park!

How soundly the dormitory slept! . . . How very still the whole large house! What was the time? I felt restless to know. There stood a clock in the classe below; what hindered me from venturing down to consult it? By such a moon, its large white face and jet-black figures must be vividly distinct . . .

On these hot July nights, close air could not be tolerated, and the chamber-door stood wide open . . . The oak staircase creaks somewhat as I descend, but not much . . .

The great classe-doors are close shut: they are bolted. On the other hand, the entrance to the corridor stands open . . . [It] offers

The Park, with the Belliard statue in the background, by. F. Stroobant
Brussels City Archives

a cheerful vista, leading to the high vestibule which opens direct upon the street.

Hush! – the clock strikes. Ghostly deep as is the stillness of this convent, it is only eleven. While my ear follows to silence the hum of the last stroke, I catch faintly from the built-out capital a sound like bells or like a band – a sound where sweetness, where victory, where mourning blend. Oh, to approach this music nearer, to listen to it alone by the rushy basin! . . .

There, in the corridor, hangs my garden-costume, my large hat, my shawl. There is no lock on the huge, heavy porte-cochère; there is no key to seek: it fastens with a sort of spring-bolt, not to be opened from the outside, but which, from within, may be noiselessly withdrawn. Can I manage it? It yields to my hand . . .

I took a route well known, and went up towards the palatial and royal Haute-Ville; thence the music I had heard, certainly floated; it was hushed now, but it might re-waken. I went on; neither band nor bell-music came to meet me; another sound replaced it, a sound like a strong tide, a great flow, deepening as I proceeded. Light broke, movement gathered, chimes pealed – to what was I coming? Entering on the level of a Grande Place, I found myself, with the suddenness of magic, plunged amidst a gay, living, joyous crowd.

Villette is one blaze, one broad illumination; the whole world seems abroad; moonlight and heaven are banished: the town, by her own flambeaux, beholds her own splendour – gay dresses, grand equipages, fine horses and gallant riders throng the bright streets. I see even scores of masks. It is a strange scene, stranger than dreams. But where is the park? – I ought to be near it. In the midst of this glare the park must be shadowy and calm – *there*, at least, are neither torches, lamps, nor crowd?

I was asking this question, when an open carriage passed me filled with known faces . . . I saw the occupants of that carriage well: me they could not see, or, at least, not know, folded close in my large shawl, screened with my straw hat . . . I saw the Count De Bassompierre; I saw my godmother, handsomely apparelled . . . I saw, too, Paulina Mary, compassed with the triple halo of her beauty, her youth, and her happiness . . . seated opposite to her I saw Graham Bretton; it was in looking up at him her aspect had caught its lustre – the light repeated in *her* eyes beamed first out of his.

It gave me strange pleasure to follow these friends viewlessly, and I *did* follow them, as I thought, to the park. I watched them alight (carriages were inadmissible) amidst new and unanticipated splendours. Lo! the iron gateway, between the stone columns, was spanned by a flaming arch built of massed stars; and, following them cautiously beneath that arch, where were they, and where was I?

In a land of enchantment, a garden most gorgeous, a plain sprinkled with coloured meteors, a forest with sparks of purple and ruby and golden fire gemming the foliage . . . [It was] a fête of which the conventual Rue Fossette had not tasted, though it had opened at dawn that morning, and was still in full vigour near midnight . . .

I lost sight of the party which, from the middle of the great square, I had followed – or, rather, they vanished like a group of apparitions. On this whole scene was impressed a dream-like character; every shape was wavering, every movement floating, every voice echo-like – half-mocking, half-uncertain. Paulina and her friends being gone, I scarce could avouch that I had really seen them; nor did I miss them as guides through the chaos, far less regret them as protectors amidst the night.

That festal night would have been safe for a very child. Half the peasantry had come in from the outlying environs of Villette, and the decent burghers were all abroad and around, dressed in their best. My straw-hat passed amidst cap and jacket, short petticoat, and long calico mantle, without, perhaps, attracting a glance; I only took the precaution to bind down the broad leaf gipsy-wise, with a supplementary ribbon; and then I felt safe as if masked.

Safe I passed down the avenues – safe I mixed with the crowd where it was deepest ... My vague aim, as I went, was to find the stone-basin, with its clear depth and green lining: of that coolness and verdure I thought, with the passionate thirst of unconscious fever. Amidst the glare, and hurry, and throng, and noise, I still secretly and chiefly longed to come on that circular mirror of crystal, and surprise the moon glassing therein her pearly front ...

Already I saw the thick-planted trees which framed this tremulous and rippled glass, when, choiring out of a glade to the right, broke such a sound as I thought might be heard if Heaven were to open – such a sound, perhaps, as *was* heard above the plain of Bethlehem, on the night of glad tidings ... There swept through these shades so full a storm of harmonies that, had no tree been near against which to lean, I think I must have dropped ... The effect was as a sea breaking into song with all its waves.

The swaying tide swept this way, and then it fell back, and I followed its retreat. It led me towards a Byzantine building – a sort of kiosk near the park's centre. Round about stood crowded thousands, gathered to a grand concert in the open air. What I had heard was, I think, a wild Jager chorus; the night, the space, the scene, and my own mood, had but enhanced the sounds and their impression.

The *Petit Bassin* in the park; drawing by Charles Vander Straeten.
Charlotte may have had this pool in mind when she described a
'stone basin' in the park in *Villette*.
Royal Library of Belgium

Here were assembled ladies, looking by this light most
beautiful ... Most of [them] occupied the little light park-chairs,
and behind and beside them stood guardian gentlemen. The outer
ranks of the crowd were made up of citizens, plebeians and police.

In this outer rank I took my place. I rather liked to find
myself the silent, unknown, consequently unaccosted neighbour
of the short petticoat and the sabot; and only the distant gazer at
the silk robe, the velvet mantle, and the plumed chapeau. Amidst
so much life and joy, too, it suited me to be alone – quite alone.

*Unseen, Lucy watches and listens in to the conversations of practically all her
acquaintances in Brussels: the Brettons and De Bassompierres, Mme Beck,
Mme Walravens ... and M. Paul. What she sees and hears convinces her
that he is not for her after all, any more than Graham was; that he is
to marry someone else, and intends to leave Brussels without even saying
goodbye. Lucy's desolation no doubt echoes that of Charlotte herself,
during her time in Brussels, hopelessly in love with a married man.*

16

CHARLOTTE'S SECOND YEAR
IN BRUSSELS

One day is like another ... I know you, living in the country can hardly believe that it is possible life can be monotonous in the centre of a brilliant capital like Brussels – but so it is – I feel it most in the holidays – when all the girls go out to visit – and it sometimes happens that I am left during several hours quite alone – with four great desolate classrooms at my disposition – I try to read, I try to write but in vain. I then wander about from room to room – but the silence and loneliness of all the house weighs down one's spirits like lead. (Letter to Ellen Nussey, June 1843)

But I must not complain. I lived in a house full of robust life; I might have had companions, and I chose solitude. (*Villette*, Chapter 14)

At the end of October 1842 Aunt Branwell, who had funded Charlotte's and Emily's study stay in Brussels, fell seriously ill. The girls made hasty preparations to return home, this time sailing from Antwerp, but it was too late to see their aunt; as they were about to leave they received the news of her death. They did not even reach Haworth in time for the funeral. In the space of two months they had lost Aunt Branwell, Martha Taylor and also their father's much-loved curate William Weightman, a favourite with all the family, who had died of cholera in September at the age of twenty-eight. 'How dreary and void everything seems,' Charlotte wrote.[1]

Emily did not go back to Belgium. Doubtless glad of an excuse to stay at the Parsonage, for she had been desperately homesick, she contentedly took her aunt's place as the family housekeeper.

Charlotte returned to the Pensionnat alone. She said later that she knew she was wrong to go back but was drawn by an 'irresistible impulse'.

From the beginning 1843 did not augur well. The scene is set in one of the first chapters of *Villette*. Lucy Snowe, at the start of her journey to 'Labassecour', arrives in London too late to find a hotel and decides to spend the night on board the *Boue-Marine* steamer, due to sail the following morning. She asks some Thames watermen to row her out to the ship. Lucy's solitude in one strange city on her way to start a new life in another, her terror at finding herself on the water at midnight, at the mercy of the foul-mouthed men who haggle over her fare, sets the tone for her solitary adventures in *Villette*. This adventure is a precise account of Charlotte's own experience when she arrived exhausted in London on the night of 27 January 1843 after the all-day train ride from Leeds.

It was a year predominantly sombre, broodingly Basse-Ville rather than bright upbeat Haute-Ville in mood, ending with a heart-broken Charlotte taking her leave of Belgium at Ostend. True, her first letters home sound quite cheerful, despite the bitterly cold

weather in the early part of the year and even though she was now a teacher as well as a pupil at the school. Teaching children was something she always found a strain. At the start of the year she had a teaching assignment more to her liking: giving English lessons to M. Heger, as well as continuing to write French essays for him. But the English classes with him were discontinued, and the French tutorials became less frequent. Moreover, as the year wore on, the friends who remained in Brussels left for pastures new. Mary Taylor had already left at the end of the previous year. The Wheelwrights and Mary Dixon moved on in the summer of 1843. Charlotte's letters became increasingly negative and embittered.

The Hegers felt that Charlotte's loneliness was her own fault. One day M. Heger gave her a lecture on the need to be more sociable. He and his wife wished that she would befriend her fellow-teachers, Mlles Blanche, Haussé and Sophie. Charlotte hated Mlle Blanche – probably the model for Zélie St Pierre in *Villette* – and did not much seek out the company of the other two, although she was not quite as dismissive of them as Lucy is of the teachers at Mme Beck's. Mlle Haussé was very possibly the inspiration for Hortense Moore in *Shirley*; if so, the portrait is humorous rather than unkind. And there seems to have been an amicable relationship with Mlle Sophie, who wrote Charlotte an affectionate note just before she left Brussels.

But none of these women were kindred spirits, and only the friendship with Heger counted for her. As long as she felt she retained it, life at the Pensionnat was bearable, but as her feelings for him intensified she found she was seeing less and less of him. She blamed Mme Heger, who she now felt was treating her coldly, for keeping him away from her. Other ex-pupils of the Pensionnat,

Opposite: London Bridge Wharf; woodcut, c. 1840. The Ostend packet or steam ship made the fourteen-hour journey to Ostend from here twice a week. In January 1843 Charlotte, returning to Brussels alone, arrived in London too late to find a hotel. She was due to sail the next day and had herself rowed out to the ship to spend the night on board.
London Metropolitan Archives

Frederika Macdonald for instance, spoke of Zoë Heger as kind, wise and motherly. It seems likely that Charlotte's alienation from her was of her own making. This experience was nothing new for her. In most of her previous teaching posts she had ended up feeling isolated and resentful towards her employers, particularly her female employers. Morbidly sensitive and touchy, she always found fault with their treatment of her.

In this case, of course, there was an additional reason for the estrangement. Doubtless Charlotte's obsession with Heger had not escaped his wife's notice, and she thought it wisest for all concerned if Charlotte saw as little of him as possible.

It is not very probable that she was jealous of this plain and awkward young Englishwoman. But she may have sensed the disturbingly obsessive nature of Charlotte's feelings. It would not have been her first experience of a schoolgirl crush, but this seemed to be something more. She had the reputation of her school to consider.

Are Charlotte's feelings for Heger best described as simply a bad case of a 'crush' – hero-worship – or as genuine adult passion? At twenty-seven, she had created fictional romantic heroes but had never before met a real-life man who attracted her. Despite her diffidence about her own powers of attraction she had received two offers of marriage, the first from a clergyman brother of Ellen Nussey's, the second from another clergyman who proposed a few days after meeting her, but she had refused both proposals.

None of the men she had encountered in her limited social circle had come close to Constantin Heger. Was she aware of anything wrong in what she felt for this married man, her employer's husband? We must look for clues to her emotions in the letters she wrote to him after leaving Brussels, in *Villette* – while remembering that it is fiction and not autobiography – and in an experience she had in the lonely summer of her lonely second year.

One day in that summer, when her mood was at its lowest, she had an odd impulse that furnished her with one of the most memorable scenes in *Villette* and was one of the most extraordinary in her life.

17

THE CONFESSION AT ST GUDULE'S

In a few days our vacations will begin – everybody is joyous and animated at the prospect because everybody is to go home – I know that I am to stay here during the 5 weeks that the holidays last and that I shall be much alone and consequently get downcast and find both days and nights of a weary length – it is the first time in my life that I have really dreaded the vacation. (Letter to Ellen Nussey, 6 August 1843)

At first I lacked courage to venture very far from the Rue Fossette, but by degrees I sought the city gates, and passed them, and then went wandering away far along chaussées, through fields, beyond cemeteries, Catholic and Protestant, beyond farmsteads, to lanes and little woods, and I know not where. A goad thrust me on, a fever forbade me to rest; a want of companionship maintained in my soul the cravings of a most deadly famine. I often walked all day, through the burning noon and the arid afternoon, and the dusk evening, and came back with moonrise. (*Villette*, Chapter 15)

'I, daughter, am Père Silas; that unworthy son of Holy Church whom you once honoured with a noble and touching confidence, showing me the core of a heart, and the inner shrine of a mind whereof, in solemn truth, I coveted the direction, in behalf of the only true faith. Nor have I for a day lost sight of you, nor for an hour failed to take in you a rooted interest. Passed under the discipline of Rome, moulded by her high training, inoculated with her salutary doctrines, inspired by the zeal she alone gives – I realize

what then might be your spiritual rank, your practical value; and I envy Heresy her prey.' (*Villette*, Chapter 34. At Mme Walravens' house Lucy runs into Père Silas, the priest who heard her confession. His words show that he has not forgotten her!)

At the same time allow me to tell you that there are some Catholics – who are as good as any Christians can be to whom the bible is a sealed book and much better than scores of Protestants. (Letter to Ellen Nussey, July 1842)

As we have seen, the Gothic Church of St Gudule was important in the history of Rue d'Isabelle, since the street's *raison d'être* was to provide the royal household with a route to it. And it was a church that came to be important in Charlotte's history, too.

From the Pensionnat garden she could hear its bells, but of course she worshipped not at the Catholic St Gudule but at the Protestant chapel in Place du Musée. Until 1 September 1843 she could never have imagined that she, a staunch Protestant and the daughter of a Protestant clergyman, would ever enter this Catholic church as anything other than a tourist. Her frequent references to Catholicism while abroad had been anything but complimentary.

Opposite: The Cathedral of St Michael and St Gudule by F. Stroobant. St Michael and St Gudule are the patron saints of Brussels. The original collegiate church on the site was dedicated to St Michael; in 1047 the relics of St Gudule were transferred there, and from then on she, too, became a patron saint of the city. She has always been the more popular, and the church is generally known as 'Sainte Gudule's'. The Gothic building was constructed from the thirteenth to fifteenth centuries, although subsequent alterations and additions have resulted in a mixture of architectural styles. The twin towers resemble those of Notre Dame in Paris, but unlike the façade of Notre Dame with its rose window St Gudule's has a pointed arch window in the Brabantine Gothic style. Often referred to over the ages as 'the Cathedral', it did not officially achieve this status until 1962. Previously Brussels came under the bishopric of Mechelen.
Royal Library of Belgium

The interior of the Cathedral; engraving by
T. Turnbull from a drawing by T. Allom, 1841
Royal Library of Belgium

To cite one example in a letter to Ellen Nussey the previous summer:

> My advice to all Protestants who are tempted to do any-
> thing so besotted as turn Catholic – is to walk over the sea
> on to the Continent – to attend mass sedulously for a time
> – to note well the mummeries thereof – also the idiotic,
> mercenary, aspect of all the priests – and *then* if they are
> still disposed to consider Papistry in any other light than a
> most feeble, childish piece of humbug let them turn Papist
> at once that's all –- I consider Methodism, Quaker-
> ism, and the extremes of High and Low Churchism
> foolish but Roman Catholicism beats them all.[1]

On that first day of September 1843 Charlotte had been practically alone at the Pensionnat – alone in Brussels, in fact – since the school broke up for the summer holidays on 15 August. The other pupils and teachers were on holiday with their families. The Hegers were in Blankenberge, today still a popular Belgian seaside resort.

Why did she not go home for the holidays? Aunt Branwell had left the three sisters some money, and she could surely have afforded the expense. Was she paralysed by inertia and depression, perhaps by reluctance to leave a place associated with M. Heger? Whatever the reason, she stayed on in the school, seeking an escape from its empty classrooms by walking all day in the streets and boulevards of Brussels and the roads leading into the countryside.

One day, after a trek to the Protestant cemetery and the fields beyond, she could not face returning to the deserted Pensionnat. To put off the evil hour she walked around for some time in the streets near the school.

She found herself in front of St Gudule's. The bell was tolling for the evening service. After hesitating for a moment she went slowly up the steps.

We know exactly what happened next because we have her account in a letter to Emily written the next day (as well as the rather different version given by Lucy Snowe in *Villette*). She stayed for the service, and when it was over she still felt she could not face going back to the school:

> An odd whim came into my head. In a solitary part of the Cathedral six or seven people still remained kneeling by the confessionals. In two confessionals I saw a priest. I felt as if I did not care what I did, provided it was not absolutely wrong, and that it served to vary my life and yield a moment's interest. I took a fancy to change myself into a Catholic and go and make a real confession to see what it was like. Knowing me as you do, you will think this odd, but when people are by themselves they have

singular fancies. A penitent was occupied in confessing. They do not go into the sort of pew or cloister which the priest occupies, but kneel down on the steps and confess through a grating. Both the confessor and the penitent whisper very low, you can hardly hear their voices. After I had watched two or three penitents go and return I approached at last and knelt down in a niche which was just vacated. I had to kneel there ten minutes waiting, for on the other side was another penitent invisible to me. At last that went away and a little wooden door inside the grating opened, and I saw the priest leaning his ear towards me. I was obliged to begin, and yet I did not know a word of the formula with which they always commence their confessions. It was a funny position. I felt precisely as I did when alone on the Thames at midnight. I commenced with saying I was a foreigner and had been brought up a Protestant. The priest asked if I was a Protestant then. I

somehow could not tell a lie and said 'yes'. He replied that in that case I could not '*jouir du bonheur de la confesse*';[2] but I was determined to confess, and at last he said he would allow me because it might be the first step towards returning to the true church. I actually did confess – a real confession. When I had done he told me his address, and said that every morning I was to go to the rue du Parc – to his house – and he would reason with me and try to convince me of the error and enormity of being a Protestant!!! I promised faithfully to go. Of course, however, the adventure stops there, and I hope I shall never see the priest again. I think you had better not tell papa of this. He will not understand that it was only a freak, and will perhaps think I am going to turn Catholic.[3]

What we do *not* know, of course, is what she confessed. Years before, in her first teaching post when she was just out of her teens, she had gone through a similar period of depression and had told her friend Ellen that she had dark thoughts she could not confess to anyone. They related to the desires that found expression in her lurid juvenile love stories dominated by excitingly saturnine Byronic heroes.

In *Villette* Lucy tells Graham Bretton that what she confessed to Père Silas, the priest, was not any specific wrongdoing but merely a 'dreary, desperate complaint'. She was depressed and just needed to talk to someone. But even if Charlotte had no specific sin on her conscience, in view of the tortured letters she later wrote to Heger it seems likely her confession was prompted by more than

Opposite: St Gudule. Legend has it that Gudule was a count's daughter who was born in the seventh century in Moorsel, a village in East Flanders. As a young woman she dedicated herself to God, led an austere life of prayer and gave generously to the poor. Before dawn each morning she would go to church from her father's castle at some distance from the village. The devil tried to blow out her lantern, and an angel was sent to light it again. She is usually depicted carrying a lamp.

just a wish for human contact and some variety in the monotony of her life. Whatever she actually told the priest, we can be fairly sure that her feelings for Heger had something to do with the depression that drove her to the confessional. Was she tormented by the kind of desires she had once hinted at to Ellen? If so, did she hint at them to the priest?

According to one tradition, the confessional at which Charlotte Brontë knelt is the second one on the left. We can go into the Cathedral and stand for a moment musing on what led her there and what she may have said. That kindly priest may have been the only person – unless she at any time made a confession to Emily or Ellen Nussey or Mary Taylor – to hear from her own lips what Frederika MacDonald, writing in 1914, was to call 'the secret of Charlotte Brontë': the real nature of her feelings for Constantin Heger.

Confessional in the Cathedral. From Louis Haghe, *Sketches in Belgium and Germany*, Volume I, 1840
Royal Library of Belgium

18

LEAVING BRUSSELS

After her confession in the church Lucy Snowe collapses in the street and is rescued by Graham Bretton, who takes her to recover in the comfort of his little château somewhere in the countryside near Villette. During a long stay with him and his mother she finds herself increasingly attracted to him but is forced to realize that the attraction is not mutual. The Graham Brettons of this world do not usually fall in love with the Lucy Snowes. Once she comes to terms with that fact, it is Paul Emanuel who gradually comes to occupy her thoughts. When she eventually finds that he reciprocates her feelings and loves her for what she is, with all her faults and physical unattractiveness, Lucy finally finds fulfilment and peace.

But no such outcome awaited Charlotte Brontë when she left St Gudule's to return to the empty school, with the prospect of many more weeks there alone. It was to be a long time before her state of mind attained anything approaching such peace and fulfilment. Her physical solitude ended when classes started up again at the end of September, but her emotional loneliness became more and more acute as it grew clear that M. Heger was avoiding her – or being kept away from her – and relations with Mme Heger grew frostier by the day. Charlotte knew she should leave but could not find the willpower to tear herself away. In October she gave notice, but Heger, presumably not suspecting the true nature of her feelings, persuaded her to stay longer and pursue her studies – just as he had kindly urged both sisters to come back for a second year for the sake of their education. She stayed on to the end of the year. But the situation became unbearable, and in December, after receiving a letter from Mary Taylor urging her to leave Brussels before she sank any deeper into inertia, she announced that she was going at the end of the year. On 1 January 1844 she left Brussels for good.

In her last days there she was pleasantly taken aback by the affection and regret expressed by at least some of her pupils when her departure was announced. This was borne out by the letters she received later from some of the girls. Replying to a former pupil called Victoire who had written to complain about the new English mistress and to beg Charlotte to return, Charlotte wrote, 'You tell me to return to Belgium – that is not possible. I cannot return to you – but I can think of you all and love you … I knew I loved my pupils – but I did not know that they had for me the affection those letters express.'[1]

It appears, then, that the unflattering picture of Belgian schoolchildren given in Charlotte's novels and her caustic comments on them when letting off steam in letters home were not the whole story of her teaching experience in Belgium.

Saying goodbye to Heger hurt terribly. His wife accompanied her to Ostend and saw her on to the boat. Charlotte is supposed to have sworn she would 'have her revenge', perhaps for being viewed with distrust by Mme Heger and kept apart from her husband in her last months at the Pensionnat.

She could be said to have taken her revenge ten years later with the publication of *Villette*, since Mme Heger was angered and upset by the depiction of her Pensionnat – easily identifiable to anyone who knew it – and what she took to be the caricature of her as Mme Beck.

In fairness it should be said that Mme Beck is a fictional creation and that Charlotte tried to limit any damage the novel might do to the Hegers not only by using fictitious place names but by trying to prevent its publication in Belgium. Given her fame by this time, though, the attempt was doomed to failure. And of course she had not envisaged dying only two years after the novel was published. French translations quickly appeared in Belgium, and Mme Heger was soon able to read it in her native language, horrified at how easily her Pensionnat would be identified from the book. There were many aspects of Mme Beck and her school to distress and outrage the directress of the Heger establishment. The ease with which young De Hamal climbs through attic windows in order to woo Ginevra might lead the parents of the demoiselles at the real school to fear similar incursions. As for Mme Beck herself, her many unlikeable qualities extend to cold-heartedness even towards her own children, let alone her staff and pupils. As Mme Heger read this former pupil-cum-assistant-teacher's fictional account of the school and its inmates, her remarks about 'Labassecour' and the 'Labassecouriens', she must have had an indignant sense of Charlotte's ingratitude towards the place and the people that had provided her with accommodation, education and employment.

Years later, the Hegers' son Paul, reading the novel for the first time, reportedly saw it as fiction rather than autobiography and was not particularly offended by it. Understandably, Zoë Heger took a less objective view. She refused for some time to admit English pupils to the school; refused to meet Brontë admirers asking to look around the Pensionnat; refused to meet Mrs Gaskell when she visited M. Heger to gather material for her biography. Charlotte's stay at the school left its mark on others apart from Charlotte herself. For the proprietress of the Pensionnat Charlotte Brontë's passage through the school was a dark episode in its long and happy history.

WE MET AS WE HAD ALWAYS MET,
AS MASTER AND PUPIL

Crimsworth with Frances Henri in her lodgings in Rue
Notre Dame aux Neiges
Edmund Dulac, illustration for The Professor, *Dent, London, 1922*

19

AFTER BRUSSELS: WRITING TO M. HEGER

But *Villette*, in which Charlotte Brontë was to transform her experiences in Belgium into art, was still a long time ahead. In the meantime, as the wind wuthered on the moors back at the Parsonage, as the months went by and as the project of opening a school came to nothing – there was not a single application from prospective pupils – the main outlet Charlotte found for her unhappiness and frustration was writing to her former teacher. At first M. Heger answered her letters. But as they became more emotional and demanding his became cooler and less frequent. He even limited the number of times she was to write to him to once every six months.

What exactly did she hope for from him? After leaving Brussels did she simply wish to retain his friendship, if only by correspondence? In letter after letter she virtually demanded this friendship from him as a right on her part, a duty on his. She told him about the emptiness of her life without it. There was little in the situation at home to satisfy or console her. She was concerned about her father's failing sight as a result of cataracts, her own sight, which she had strained through years of writing in a tiny hand and copying engravings, and Branwell's addiction to drink and his consequent degeneration after being fired from a post as tutor. She told Heger that he was the only person she could call her 'master', the only one who had taken the trouble to nurture her talent. If she ever wrote a book, she said, she would dedicate it to him.

But she also told him how badly she needed his support as a friend. The tone of her letters, however, strongly suggests that for her he was rather more than a teacher and friend, that he was also the man she was in love with – the first man she had fallen in love with. To reach our own conclusions about what she felt for him and what she wanted from him, we can read her surviving letters to Brussels.

In one of them she says:

> Monsieur, the poor do not need a great deal to live on – they ask only the crumbs of bread which fall from the rich man's table – but if they are refused these crumbs – they die of hunger – No more do I need a great deal of affection from those I love – I would not know what to do with a whole and complete friendship – I am not accustomed to it – but you showed a *little* interest in me in days gone by when I was your pupil in Brussels – and I cling to the preservation of this *little* interest – I cling to it as I would cling on to life.

In the same letter, written almost exactly a year after taking leave of him in Brussels, she tells him of her despair when he does not reply.

> Day and night I find neither rest nor peace. If I sleep I am disturbed by tormenting dreams in which I see you . . .[1]

Ten months later her state of mind is no calmer.

> I have tried to forget you . . . I have done everything, I have sought occupations, I have absolutely forbidden myself the pleasure of speaking about you – even to Emily, but I have not been able to overcome either my regrets or my impatience – and that is truly humiliating – not to know how to get the mastery over one's own thoughts, to be the slave of

Postscript in English in the last of Charlotte's four extant letters
to Heger, dated 18 November 1845
British Library

a regret, a memory, the slave of a dominant and fixed idea
which has become a tyrant over one's mind. Why cannot I
have for you exactly as much friendship as you have for me –
neither more nor less? Then I would be so tranquil, so free –
I could keep silence for ten years without effort . . .

Writing to an old pupil cannot be a very interesting
occupation for you – I know that – but for me it is life

itself. Your last letter has sustained me – has nourished me for six months – now I need another . . . To forbid me to write to you, to refuse to reply to me – that will be to tear from me the only joy I have on earth.[2]

But no more crumbs of comfort came from Brussels. M. Heger stopped replying to her letters.

Haworth Parsonage
Brontë Parsonage Museum

CHARLOTTE'S LETTERS TO CONSTANTIN HEGER

He was mute as is the grave, he stood stirless as a tower;
At last I looked up, and saw I prayed to stone:
I asked help of that which to help had no power,
I sought love where love was utterly unknown.
(From Charlotte Brontë's poem 'He Saw My Heart's Woe')

*This English translation of Charlotte's four extant letters to Heger
is taken from Volume I of Margaret Smith's edition of the letters
of Charlotte Brontë (Oxford, 1995). In some of these letters Charlotte
refers to others she wrote to him that have not survived. None of his replies
have been preserved. The appearance of the original manuscripts of the
letters, kept in the British Library, is remarkable. At some stage three
of them were torn up and then stitched or, in one case, stuck together again
(for the probable explanation and the history of the letters as far as we
know it see Chapter 21); Charlotte's small, neat handwriting contrasts with
the untidy jagged lines where the sheets were torn. More remarkable still
are the words she wrote to her former tutor in those years when her
thoughts were constantly travelling from the Parsonage to the Pensionnat
and Brussels*

24 July 1844

*The earliest of the letters is long and chatty. This one was torn up and stuck
together again with glued strips of paper.*

Monsieur,

I am well aware that it is not my turn to write to you, but since Mrs Wheelwright is going to Brussels and is willing to take charge of a letter – it seems to me that I should not neglect such a favourable opportunity for writing to you.

I am very pleased that the school year is almost over and that the holiday period is approaching – I am pleased about it on your account, Monsieur – for I have been told that you are working too hard and that as a result your health has deteriorated a little – That is why I refrain from uttering a single complaint about your long silence – I would rather remain six months without hearing from you than add an atom to the burden – already too heavy – which overwhelms you – I well remember that it is now the time for compositions, that it will soon be the time for examinations and after that for prizes – and for the whole period you are condemned to breathe in the deadening aridity of the classes – to wear yourself out – in explaining, questioning, speaking all day long, and then in the evening you have all those dreary compositions to read, correct, almost re-write – Ah Monsieur! I once wrote you a letter which was hardly rational, because sadness was wringing my heart, but I shall do so no more – I will try to stop being egotistical and though I look on your letters as one of the greatest joys I know, I shall wait patiently to receive them until it pleases and suits you to send them. But all the same I can still write you a little letter from time to time – you have given me permission to do so.

I am very much afraid of forgetting French, for I am quite convinced that I shall see you again one day – I don't know how or when – but it must happen since I so long for it, and then I would not like to stay silent in your presence – it would be too sad to see you and not be able to speak to you; to prevent this misfortune – every single day, I learn by heart half a page of French from a book in a colloquial style: and I take pleasure in learning this lesson, Monsieur – when I pronounce the French words I seem to be chatting with you.

I have just been offered a position as principal teacher in a large boarding school in Manchester, with a salary of £100, i.e. 2,500 francs a year – I cannot accept it – because acceptance would mean having to leave my father and that cannot be – Nevertheless I have made a plan: (when one lives in seclusion one's brain is always active – one longs to be busy – one longs to launch out into an active career). Our Parsonage is a fairly large house – with some alterations – there will be room for five or six boarders – if I could find that number of children from respectable families – I would devote myself to their education – Emily is not very fond of teaching but she would nevertheless take care of the housekeeping, and though she is rather withdrawn she has too kind a heart not to do her utmost for the well-being of the children – she is also a very generous soul; and as for order, economy, strict organization – hard work – all very essential matters in a boarding school – I willingly make myself responsible for them.

There is my plan, Monsieur, which I have already explained to my father and which he considers a good one. – So all that remains is to find the pupils – a rather difficult matter – for we live a long way from towns and people hardly wish to take the trouble of crossing the mountains which form a barrier round us – but the task which lacks difficulty almost lacks merit – it is very rewarding to surmount obstacles – I do not say that I shall succeed but I shall *try* to succeed – the effort alone will do me good I fear nothing so much as idleness – lack of employment – inertia – lethargy of the faculties – when the body is idle, the spirit suffers cruelly. I would not experience this lethargy if I could write – once upon a time I used to spend whole days, weeks, complete months in writing and not quite in vain since Southey and Coleridge – two of our best authors, to whom I sent some manuscripts were pleased to express their approval of them – but at present my sight is too weak for writing – if I wrote a lot I would become blind. This weakness of sight is a terrible privation for me – without it, do you know what I would do, Monsieur? – I would write a book and I would dedicate it to my literature master – to the only master that I have ever had – to you Monsieur. I have often told you in French how much I respect you – how much I am indebted to your kindness, to your advice, I would like to tell you for once in English – That cannot be – it must not be thought of – a literary career is closed to me – only that of teaching is open to me – it does not offer the same attractions – never mind, I shall enter upon it and if I do not go far in it, it will not be for want of diligence. You too, Monsieur – you wanted to be a barrister – fate or Providence has made you a teacher – you are happy in spite of that.

Please assure Madame of my esteem – I am afraid that Maria, Louise and Claire will have already forgotten me – Prospère and Victorine have never known me well – I myself clearly remember all five – especially Louise – she had so much character – so much naïveté – so much *truthfulness* in her little face –

Goodbye Monsieur –

Your grateful pupil,

C. Brontë

[P.S.] I have not asked you to write to me soon because I don't want to seem importunate – but you are too good to forget that I wish it all the same – yes – I wish for it very much – that is enough – after all, do as you please, Monsieur – if in fact I received a letter and thought that you had written it *out of pity* for me – that would hurt me very much.

It seems that Mrs Wheelwright is going to Paris before going to Brussels – but she will put my letter in the post at Boulogne – once more goodbye, Monsieur – it hurts to say goodbye even in a letter – Oh it is certain that I shall see you again one day – it really has to be – for as soon as I have earned enough money to go to Brussels I shall go – and I shall see you again if it is only for a moment.

24 October 1844

The second letter, written in haste, is much shorter. This one was torn up and the pieces stitched together. The word 'respect' towards the end replaces another ('affection') that has been crossed out.

Monsieur,

I am full of joy this morning – something which has rarely happened to me these last two years – it is because a gentleman of my acquaintance [Joe Taylor] will be passing through Brussels and has offered to take charge of a letter to you – which either he or else his sister will deliver to you, so that I shall be certain you have received it.

I am not going to write a long letter – first of all I haven't the time – it has to go immediately – and then I am afraid of bothering you. I would just like to ask you whether you heard from me at the beginning of May and then in the month of August? For all those six months I have been expecting a letter from you, Monsieur – six months of waiting – is a very long time indeed! Nevertheless I am not complaining and I shall be richly recompensed for a little sadness – if you are now willing to write a letter and give it to this gentleman – or to his sister – who would deliver it to me without fail.

However short the letter may be I shall be satisfied with it – only do not forget to tell me how you are, Monsieur, and how Madame and the children are and the teachers and pupils.

My father and sister send you their regards – my father's affliction is gradually increasing – however he is still not completely blind – my sisters are keeping well but my poor brother is always ill.

Goodbye Monsieur, I am counting on soon having news of you – this thought delights me for the remembrance of your kindness will never fade from my memory and so long as this remembrance endures the respect it has inspired in me will endure also.

Your very devoted pupil,

C. Brontë

[P.S.] I have just had bound all the books that you gave me when I was still in Brussels. I take pleasure in looking at them – they make quite a little library – First there are the complete works of Bernardin de St Pierre – the Pensées of Pascale – a book of verse, two German books – and (something worth all the rest)

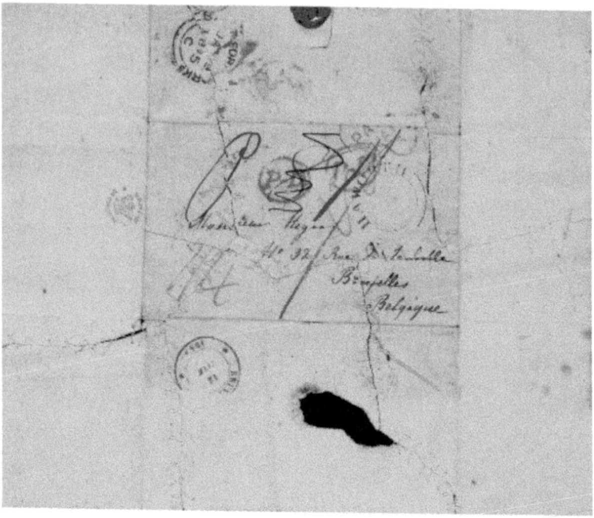

Monsieur Wegner
N° 32 Rue de Louvain
Bruxelles
Belgique

Mr Taylor est revenu ... je lui ai promis ... il ... ... bien ... pour ... ... dès ... la ... l'indépendance. Mademoiselle Ma Taylor est revenue. Je n'ai pu ... tenir ... de la part de Monsieur Wegner dit elle ... lettre ... message.

Ayant bien ... que ... je me suis dit, ce que je voudrais à un autre en pareille circonstance. Il faut être toujours et surtout, ne pas être affligé d'un malheur que l'on ne voy pas ... ... j'ai ... efforcé à me faire plaisir à ... ... plaindre ...

... ... quand on ... se plaint pas et que ... sent se ... toujours les feuilles ... ... et ... fait les ... ... jusque insupportable.

... et ... je ... trouve ... repos ni joie ... je ... je fais des vœux ... ... vous ... toujours tristes toujours semblables et inter tendre moi.

Pardonnez-moi mon ... si je prends la liberté de vous écrire encore ... Comment fais je supporter la ...

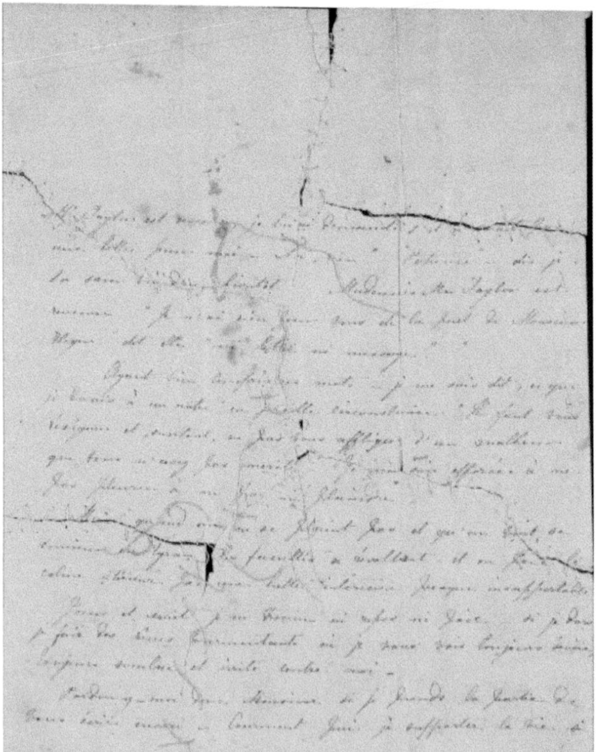

two speeches, by Professor Heger – given at the Prize Distribution of the Athénée Royal.

8 January 1845

The third letter has also been torn up and then stitched together. After the sentence 'One suffers in silence so long as one has the strength and when that strength fails one speaks without measuring one's words too much' there are two lines that are so heavily scored out they are illegible, after which Charlotte ends with the formulaic 'I wish Monsieur happiness and prosperity'.

Mr Taylor returned. I asked him if he had a letter for me – 'No, nothing.' 'Patience' – I say – 'His sister will be coming soon' – Miss Taylor returned 'I have nothing for you from M. Heger' she says 'neither letter nor message.'

When I had taken in the full meaning of these words – I said to myself, what I would say to someone else in such a case 'You will have to resign yourself to the fact, and above all, not distress yourself about a misfortune that you have not deserved.' I did my utmost not to cry not to complain –

But when one does not complain, and when one wants to master oneself with a tyrant's grip – one's faculties rise in revolt – and one pays for outward calm by an almost unbearable inward struggle.

Day and night I find neither rest nor peace – if I sleep I have tormenting dreams in which I see you always severe, always saturnine and angry with me –

Forgive me then Monsieur if I take the step of writing to you again – How can I bear my life unless I make an effort to alleviate its sufferings?

Opposite: Envelope and page of one of the three letters of Charlotte's that were torn up and later repaired. According to Heger's daughter Louise, they were thrown away by her father and then retrieved, repaired and kept by Mme Heger. This one is dated 8 January 1845.
British Library

I know that you will lose patience with me when you read this letter – You will say that I am over-excited – that I have black thoughts etc. So be it Monsieur – I do not seek to justify myself, I submit to all kinds of reproaches – all I know – is that I cannot – that I will not resign myself to the total loss of my master's friendship – I would rather undergo the greatest bodily pains than have my heart constantly lacerated by searing regrets. If my master withdraws his friendship from me entirely I shall be absolutely without hope – if he gives me a little friendship – a very little – I shall be content – happy, I would have a motive for living – for working.

Monsieur, the poor do not need a great deal to live on – they ask only the crumbs of bread which fall from the rich men's table – but if they are refused these crumbs – they die of hunger – No more do I need a great deal of affection from those I love – I would not know what to do with a whole and complete friendship - I am not accustomed to it – but you showed a *little* interest in me in days gone by when I was your pupil in Brussels – and I cling to the preservation of this *little* interest - I cling to it as I would cling on to life.

Perhaps you will say to me – 'I no longer take the slightest interest in you Miss Charlotte – you no longer belong to my household – I have forgotten you.'

Well Monsieur tell me so candidly – it will be a shock to me – that doesn't matter – it will still be less horrible than uncertainty.

I don't want to re-read this letter – I am sending it as I have written it – Nevertheless I am as it were dimly aware that there are some cold and rational people who would say on reading it – 'she is raving' – My sole revenge is to wish these people – a single day of the torments that I have suffered for eight months – then we should see whether they wouldn't be raving too.

One suffers in silence so long as one has the strength and when that strength fails one speaks without measuring one's words too much.

I wish Monsieur happiness and prosperity.

18 November 1845

In this letter, the last one we have, Charlotte refers to one she wrote in
May 1845 that has not survived. She also refers to one of Heger's that she says
has sustained her for six months. In the margin of the last sheet someone,
presumably Heger, has scribbled what appears to be the address
of a Brussels shoemaker. This is the only letter that hasn't been torn up.
The neatly written pages are intact. The same cannot be said of Charlotte's
state of mind when she wrote them. The postscript is in English.

Monsieur,

The six months of silence have elapsed; today is the 18th November,
my last letter was dated (I believe) the 18th May; therefore I can
write to you again without breaking my promise.

The summer and autumn have seemed very long to me; to
tell the truth I have had to make painful efforts to endure until now
the privation I imposed on myself: you, Monsieur – you cannot
conceive what that means – but imagine for a moment that one of
your children is separated from you by a distance of 160 leagues,
and that you have to let six months go by without writing to him,
without receiving news of him, without hearing him spoken of,
without knowing how he is, then you will easily understand what
hardship there is in such an obligation. I will tell you candidly
that during this time of waiting I have tried to forget you, for the
memory of a person one believes one is never to see again, and
whom one nevertheless greatly respects, torments the mind exceed-
ingly and when one has suffered this kind of anxiety for one or two
years, one is ready to do anything to regain peace of mind. I have
done everything, I have sought occupations, I have absolutely forbidden myself the pleasure of speaking about you – even to Emily,
but I have not been able to overcome either my regrets or my impatience – and that is truly humiliating – not to know how to get
the mastery over one's own thoughts, to be the slave of a regret, a
memory, the slave of a dominant and fixed idea which has become
a tyrant over one's mind. Why cannot I have for you exactly as

much friendship as you have for me – neither more nor less? Then I would be so tranquil, so free – I could keep silence for ten years without effort.

My father is well but his sight has almost gone, he can no longer read or write; nevertheless the doctors' advice is to wait a few months longer before attempting an operation – for him the winter will be nothing but a long night – he rarely complains, I admire his patience – if Providence ordains that the same calamity should be my own fate – may He at least grant me as much patience to endure it! It seems to me, Monsieur, that what is most bitterly painful in great bodily afflictions is that we are compelled to make all those who surround us sharers in our sufferings; we can hide the troubles of the soul, but those which attack the body and destroy its faculties cannot be hidden. My father now lets me read to him and write for him, he also shows more confidence in me than he has ever done before, and that is a great consolation.

Monsieur, I have a favour to ask you; when you reply to this letter, talk to me a little about yourself – not about me, for I know that if you talk to me about myself it will be to scold me, and this time I would like to see your kindly aspect; talk to me then about your children; your forehead never had a severe look when Louise and Clare and Prospère were near you. Tell me also something about the School, the pupils, the teachers – are Mesdemoiselles Blanche, Sophie and Justine still in Brussels? Tell me where you travelled during the holidays – haven't you been through the Rhineland? Haven't you visited Cologne or Coblenz? In a word, tell me what you will, my master, but tell me something. Writing to a former assistant teacher (no, – I don't want to remember my position as an assistant teacher, I disown it) well then, writing to an old pupil cannot be a very interesting occupation for you – I know that – but for me it is life itself. Your last letter has sustained me – has nourished me for six months – now I need another and you will give it me – not because you have any friendship for me – you cannot have much – but because you have a compassionate soul and because you would not condemn anyone to undergo long suffering in order to spare yourself a few moments of tedium. To forbid me to write to you, to refuse to reply to me – that will be to tear from me the only joy I have on earth – to deprive me of my last remaining privilege – a privilege which I will never consent to renounce voluntarily. Believe me, my master, in writing to me you do a good deed – so long as I think you are fairly pleased with me, so long as I still have the hope of hearing from you, I can be tranquil and not too sad, but when a dreary and prolonged silence seems to warn me that my master is becoming estranged from me – when day after day I await a letter and day after day disappointment flings me down again into overwhelming misery, when the sweet delight of seeing your writing and reading your counsel flees from me like an empty vision – then I am in a fever – I lose my appetite and my sleep – I pine away.

May I write to you again next May? I would have liked to wait a full year – but it is impossible – it is too long –

C. Brontë

[P.S.] I must say one word to you in English – I wish I could write to you more cheerful letters, for when I read this over, I find it to be somewhat gloomy – but forgive me my dear master – do not be irritated at my sadness – according to the words of the Bible: 'Out of the fullness of the heart, the mouth speaketh and truly I find it difficult to be cheerful so long as I think I shall never see you more. You will perceive by the defects in this letter that I am forgetting the French language – yet I read all the French books I can get, and learn daily a portion by heart – but I have never heard French spoken but once since I left Brussels – and then it sounded like music in my ears – every word was most precious to me because it reminded me of you – I love French for your sake with all my heart and soul.

Farewell my dear Master – may God protect you with special care and crown you with peculiar blessings.

C.B.

Writing, after Charlotte's death, to Ellen Nussey, who had corresponded with him about her wish to publish around five hundred of Charlotte's private letters, Heger objected on the grounds that this would not be fair to Charlotte as it would expose her 'pauvre coeur malade', her 'poor sick heart'. In the draft of his letter he crossed out 'malade' and replaced it with 'blessé' (hurt, wounded), before deciding to let the original word stand. Both words seem equally apt. The irregular tear lines down the manuscript sheets, criss-crossed by white threads, look like long jagged wounds. It was to be a long time before the scars healed, if they ever did.

21

AFTER BRUSSELS: FAME

After a time, then, there was silence from the Pensionnat. At the Parsonage Charlotte's state of depression continued for months on end. She had given up on the school plan. She had no job prospects and no marriage prospects; at nearly thirty she considered herself unmarriageable. She felt she had achieved nothing.

It was a low point in the fortunes of the family generally. In the summer of 1845 both Anne and Branwell left their teaching posts, Branwell in disgrace, apparently owing to a romantic involvement with his employer's wife. This meant that all four siblings were now at home and jobless. Branwell sank into depression, took to drink and narcotics and deteriorated rapidly. Patrick was almost blind as a result of cataracts, which were eventually operated on the following year. He now had a helpful new curate, Arthur Bell Nicholls, but apart from the late Mr Weightman, who had charmed them all, Charlotte had never taken much interest in her father's curates except as figures of fun.

Then, one day in the autumn of 1845, she came across some of Emily's poems and thought them so good she conceived a new money-earning plan for her sisters and herself that was much more appealing than teaching: to realize their long-standing dream of becoming published authors.

In 1846 Charlotte, Emily and Anne paid for the publication of a book of their poems. Two copies were sold. They decided to try novel-writing instead.

In 1847 Charlotte's *Jane Eyre*, Emily's *Wuthering Heights* and Anne's *Agnes Grey* were published under the pseudonyms of Currer,

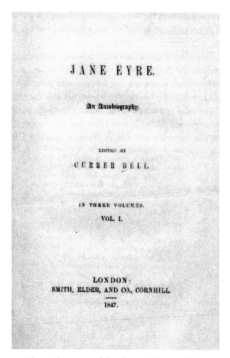

The title page of the first edition of *Jane Eyre* by 'Currer Bell'

Ellis and Acton Bell. Charlotte's first novel, *The Professor*, about a teacher in Brussels, written in 1845–6, had been rejected, but *Jane Eyre*, written at speed immediately afterwards, became an instant best-seller. *Wuthering Heights*, slower to please the public at first, in time achieved equal or even greater fame.

In September 1848 Branwell Brontë died.

In December 1848 Emily Brontë died.

In May 1849 Anne Brontë died. In the same year, despite loneliness and despair, Charlotte finished *Shirley*, her novel with a Yorkshire setting and, somewhat incongruously, a half-Belgian hero. (A more minor character in the book is the clergyman Mr Macarthey, a portrayal of the real-life Haworth curate Mr Nicholls, who was gratified at this brief appearance in the novel.)

The year 1853 saw the publication of *Villette*, in which

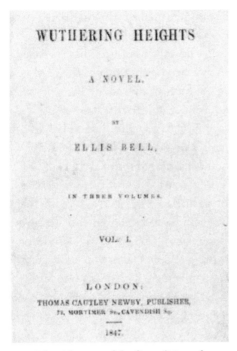

The title page of the first edition of
Wuthering Heights by 'Ellis Bell'

Charlotte perhaps finally wrote M. Heger out of her system. However, even when she announced her engagement to Rev. Arthur Nicholls soon afterwards, some of her friends wondered whether 'M. Paul' was the real love of Charlotte's life.

In 1855 Charlotte, now pregnant, died after a brief nine months of marriage in which, rather to her own surprise, she found happiness as the wife of Rev. Nicholls.

In 1857 her friend Elizabeth Gaskell published her *Life of Charlotte Brontë*. The same year also saw the posthumous publication of *The Professor*. Before reading the novel Mrs Gaskell, who knew at least something of Charlotte's feelings for Heger, was apprehensive, fearing that it would reveal too much. She was relieved to find that it did not give away Charlotte's secret.

In 1913 the complete text of Charlotte's four extant letters to M. Heger was published for the first time, revealing the full significance of her time at the Pensionnat.

The story of how the four letters have survived is an extraordinary one. As we have seen, three of them were at some stage torn up while the fourth suffered the indignity of being used by Heger to jot down the address of a shoemaker.

In old age Heger's daughter Louise (who was probably the model for little 'Georgette' in *Villette*) told Marion Spielmann, an English friend who arranged for the letters to be handed over to the British Museum, that three of them were torn into pieces by Heger as soon as he had read them and then retrieved from the wastepaper basket by his wife, who glued or stitched them together again and hid them away for fifty years. Why did she go to all this trouble? According to Spielmann, who wrote an article reporting what Louise remembered being told by her mother,[1] Mme Heger feared that Charlotte's obsession with her husband might drive her to do something to harm the reputation of the family or the school. She therefore kept the letters as evidence that there had been nothing wrong on Heger's side in his relations with his ex-pupil. If, as Louise claimed, they were torn up and rescued as soon as they were received, before Charlotte became a world-famous author, no one could have had an inkling at that time of their future interest to literary biographers.

According to Spielmann's report, when Louise showed the letters to her father after her mother's death, fifty years after they were written, he threw them away a second time and they were once again retrieved from the wastepaper basket – this time by Louise.

Spielmann's account, based on Louise's memory of events in the distant past, may have contained certain inaccuracies.[2] Some things are a little hard to understand. For example, Heger showed the letters to Mrs Gaskell when she visited him in 1856 to research her *Life of Charlotte Brontë*, which appears to contradict Louise's claim that Mme Heger hid them away. And would he not have found it rather awkward to account for the fact that they had been torn up? Perhaps he simply read them to her or used transcriptions.

Mrs Gaskell included only a few innocuous extracts from the letters in her biography. She very possibly read the complete text and was aware of the nature of Charlotte's feelings, but there was no hint of them in the *Life*. As a friend of Charlotte's, and as a Victorian biographer, it was out of the question for Elizabeth Gaskell to publish letters so revelatory and so at odds with the 'respectable' image of Charlotte she wished to present. Besides which there were too many people who would be hurt by them – not just the Hegers but Arthur Nicholls who lived until 1906.

Heger's conduct was similarly discreet and showed sensitivity. If it was indeed he who tore the letters up, one motive may surely have been the sense that it would not be right to keep disclosures Charlotte might well blush to recall one day, quite apart from any awkwardness he felt himself as their recipient. Although he outlived her by forty years he refused to allow their publication, to protect her privacy as much as his own. It was not until 1913, after his death and that of Mr Nicholls, that Heger's children decided to hand them over to the British Museum. Their publication that year made known an aspect of Charlotte's emotional life hitherto only speculated about on the basis of *Villette*, and prompted new interest in her years in Brussels. There was a spate of biographical and critical works such as Frederika Macdonald's *The Secret of Charlotte Brontë*, which argued that Charlotte's unrequited love for her 'professor' broke her heart but was what gave her writing its passion and romance.

Since 1913 Brontë biographers have given due importance to the role played by Brussels and M. Heger in Charlotte's life. They may differ in their analysis of her feelings for him, but there is general agreement that her time at the Pensionnat was pivotal in making her the person and writer she became.

Charlotte by George Richmond, 1850
National Portrait Gallery

22

THE PENSIONNAT BECOMES
A PLACE OF PILGRIMAGE

Even before the revelation of the Brontë-Heger letters readers of *Villette* could not be unaware of the significance of Brussels for Charlotte. Until the Pensionnat was demolished in 1909 it was a place of pilgrimage for admirers of the novel, even if their numbers were never anything like the hordes who made the journey to Haworth. Many of the Brussels pilgrims came from the United States, where Charlotte's last novel enjoyed a popularity it never knew in Britain. They would take in the city as part of their European tour, setting out from their hotel with a copy of *Villette* or *The Professor* under their arm to seek Madame Beck's Pensionnat de Demoiselles. These hopeful tourists usually succeeded without much trouble in locating General Belliard's statue and descending the steps behind it. Once at the door of the Pensionnat they not infrequently summoned up the courage to ring the bell. And not infrequently the person giving them a guided tour round the classrooms where Charlotte and Emily had sat was a member of the Heger family. When M. and Mme Heger grew too old to run the school it was taken over by their daughters.

Adeline Trafton, an American who visited Brussels in the 1860s, describes locating the Belliard steps with a party of young friends:

> We descended into the narrow, noiseless street and stood,
> – an awe-struck group, – before the great square house,
> upon the door-plate of which we read, – 'Pensionnat de
> Demoiselles. Heger-Parent'.[1]

The door was opened by a teacher who, it turned out, had been a pupil there at the same time as Charlotte and Emily. Although her comments showed she had scant admiration for Charlotte or her books, she good-humouredly led the excited girls through the classrooms and into the garden where she gave them leaves from the pear trees as souvenirs, which they showed to their parents back at the hotel as proof that their adventure really had taken place.

Over the years, literary visitors to the school enthusiastically identifying landmarks of Lucy Snowe's Pensionnat ('That's the Allée Défendue! That's the pear-tree walk!') were sometimes startled by the sudden appearance of M. Heger announcing, 'Et moi, je suis Monsieur Paul!'

The last pilgrims to go inside the Pensionnat before its demolition have left haunting accounts. By this time the Heger daughters had moved their establishment to smart Avenue Louise and the Pensionnat building had since been used by a local day school and also for adult education. But even in its final days, when it was standing empty and the garden had deteriorated sadly since the summer evenings when M. Heger tended the vines and watered the rose-bushes, its last visitors had no difficulty in recognizing it as the school in *Villette*. One of these was the British critic Gerald Cumberland, who had to bribe the caretaker to let him into the doomed building. Wandering alone in the Allée Défendue as twilight descended, he had an even more powerful sense of communion with the spirits of Charlotte and Emily Brontë than he had felt on the moors of Haworth.[2] Months later the school had gone the way of the rest of the quarter. From now on it existed only in the pages of *Villette*.

What was the special appeal of Brussels and the Pensionnat for these literary pilgrims? Of course there has always been a particular fascination in the Brontës, in any place associated with them, any new light shed on them. But the Pensionnat was particularly fascinating because it is depicted so vividly in *Villette*. We feel we know the school in Brussels in more intimate detail than any other place in a Brontë novel. For the Brussels Brontë pilgrims there was also the thrill of feeling themselves members of a select band. Even at the height of its popularity *Villette's* following was small compared with that of *Wuthering Heights* or *Jane Eyre*. There was the excitement of being not just a pilgrim but a detective, seeking out traces in a site far removed from the well-worn track of pilgrimage to the door of the Parsonage. These Brussels detective-pilgrims were intrigued, above all, by the sheer incongruity of Charlotte and Emily's Belgian adventure in an urban, foreign location so different in every way from their native Yorkshire.

The publication of the letters to Heger in 1913 confirmed what readers of *Villette* had always suspected, namely that although, thanks to the Brontë legacy, the Yorkshire moors are popularly seen as the fitting backdrop for hopeless passion, Charlotte Brontë's own hopeless passion had a totally different setting – the place she called in *The Professor* 'unromantic, unpoetic Belgium'.[3]

The Pensionnat, *c.* 1910. This is the last photo taken of it before
it was demolished.
Brontë Parsonage Museum

173

The Brussels Pensionnat and the experience of living in Belgium were in some important respects as formative for Charlotte as Haworth Parsonage. As Marion Spielmann put it in an article called *Charlotte Brontë in Brussels* written in 1916, the centenary of her birth, Charlotte Brontë was in many ways 'the product of the Rue d'Isabelle'. [4]

Arthur Bell Nicholls (1819–1906). He and Charlotte were married in 1854. He had been her father's curate since 1845. From a photograph dated *c.* 1867.
Brontë Parsonage Museum

TIMELINE

1842

8 February: Charlotte and Emily set off for Brussels, travelling by train from Leeds to London with their father Patrick, Charlotte's friend Mary Taylor and Mary's brother Joe.

12 February: After a few days' sightseeing in London the party boarded the steamship for Ostend.

14 February: After a couple of nights in an Ostend hotel they travelled by stagecoach to Brussels.

15 February: Patrick left his daughters at the Pensionnat Heger.

26(?) March: The Brontës visited Mary and Martha Taylor at their school in Koekelberg in the outskirts of the city.

28 March: Birth of Mme Heger's fourth child and first son, Prospère.

Spring and summer: In her few surviving letters from this period Charlotte reported enjoying her studies and feeling contented in Brussels.

15 August – end September: Charlotte and Emily spent the summer vacation at the Pensionnat with a few other boarders, including the Wheelwright sisters, with whom they became friendly.

12 October: Death of Martha Taylor.

29 October: Death of Aunt Branwell.

6 November: Charlotte and Emily, having heard the news of their aunt's death, returned to Haworth, sailing from Antwerp.

17 November: Death of Julia, the youngest of the Wheelwright girls.

1843

27 January: Charlotte, returning to Brussels alone, took the train to London. She sailed from London Bridge Wharf to Ostend that night and at noon the next day caught a train to Brussels, arriving in the evening.

February–March: Bitterly cold weather in Brussels with heavy snow. Charlotte was now giving classes at the Pensionnat. She also gave English lessons to M. Heger.

4 June: In a homework assignment Charlotte reported going on an outing to the country with another teacher and some of the pupils from the school, returning along the popular Brussels promenade the Allée Verte.

15 August: Start of the school summer holiday, which was to be a lonely time for Charlotte. On the same day there was a concert in the park that may have provided inspiration for the one described in *Villette*.

1 September: Charlotte's confession in the Cathedral.

18 September: Charlotte caught a glimpse of Queen Victoria on a visit to Belgium.

24 September: There was a concert in the park to mark the anniversary of the 1830 revolution, which included a performance by a huge choir. Like the park concert on 15 August, this may have inspired the description of an outdoor choral performance in *Villette*.

October: Early in October Charlotte, increasingly lonely and depressed at the Pensionnat, gave notice that she wished to resign her teaching post and return to England but was persuaded by M. Heger to stay longer.

15 November: Birth of Mme Heger's fifth child, Julie.

10 December: Charlotte attended a concert at the Salle de la Grande Harmonie and saw Leopold I and his Queen. Shortly after this she told the Hegers that she had decided to leave Brussels.

1844

1 January: Charlotte left Brussels for Ostend, arriving back in Haworth on 3 January.

Fighting on the Belliard steps during the Belgian Revolution
Reproduced in Jacques Dubreucq, Bruxelles 1000: Une histoire capitale,
published by the author, Brussels, 1999

A BRONTË WALK IN BRUSSELS

Note: for fuller information on the places referred to, see earlier chapters, in particular Chapter 3: The Site of the Pensionnat Heger Today, Chapter 9: A Look Back at the History of the Isabelle Quarter, Chapter 10: The Fate of the Isabelle Quarter and What You Can Still See and Chapter 11: Around Place Royale.

The Belliard Steps

Get off the metro at Parc and walk along Rue Royale towards Place Royale. On the right-hand side you will see a statue of General Augustin Daniel Belliard (1769–1832) who as the French ambassador to Belgium played a key role in the negotiations on Belgian independence after the 1830 revolution against Dutch rule. In 1832 he died of a stroke in the park near this spot, and the statue, the first official one in the city after independence, was erected by public subscription in 1836 in gratitude for his services. The sculptor was Guillaume Geefs, who was responsible for many notable works of the period including the monument in Place des Martyrs to the fallen of the revolution.

The building to your left as you look at the statue is the Hôtel Errera, which was here in the Brontës' time. It is currently occupied by the Flemish regional government.

Go to the top of the double staircase leading down behind the statue. In the Brontës' time a single set of steps, long, steep and rather dark, led down to the Rue d'Isabelle, which was at a lower level than the present street. It ran parallel to Rue Royale,

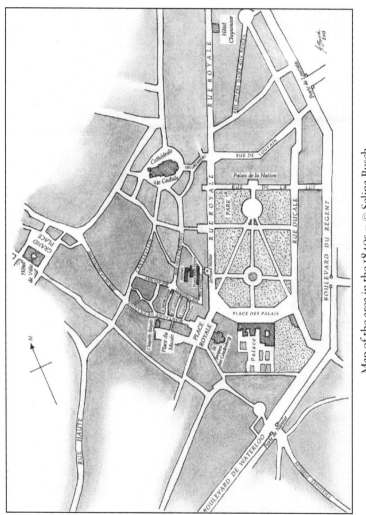

Map of the area in the 1840s — © Selina Busch

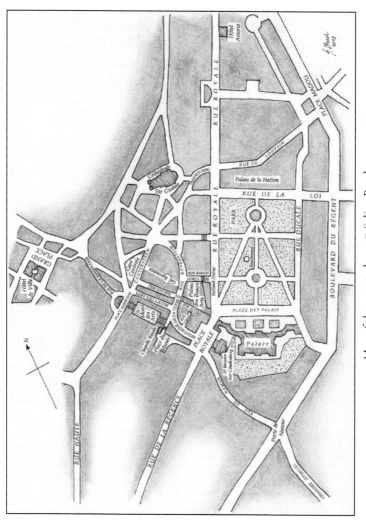

Map of the area today – © Selina Busch

and the door of the Pensionnat Heger, the boarding-school where the Brontës stayed, was immediately opposite you when you reached the bottom of the steps. In Chapter 7 of *The Professor* the hero William Crimsworth describes looking down from the top of a 'great staircase . . . into a narrow back street, which I afterwards learnt was called the Rue d'Isabelle' and seeing the door of the school where he is later to work. It was an exact description of the view of the real Pensionnat from the top of the steps.

Rue Baron Horta and 'Bozar'

Go down the steps to Rue Baron Horta. This street was built in the early years of the twentieth century when Rue d'Isabelle, together with many other charming narrow cobbled streets around the Pensionnat, was razed for redevelopment projects such as the Mont des Arts complex and the construction of the Gare Centrale on the rail link between the North and South Stations.

The Pensionnat was demolished in 1909–10. The school classrooms stood roughly on the site of the BNP Paribas Fortis Bank building to your right as you walk up Rue Baron Horta, while the garden was in the area now occupied by the Palais des Beaux-Arts arts centre on the left.

The Palais des Beaux-Arts ('Bozar') is a 1920s Art Deco building designed by the architect Victor Horta (1861–1947), after whom the street is named, who was famed for the Art Nouveau creations of his earlier period. The sloping and irregular terrain of the site posed an architectural challenge, as did the height restrictions imposed to preserve the view of Brussels from the Royal Palace. Horta got round these problems by creating eight different levels inside the building, some of them underground. Bozar is home to the National Orchestra of Belgium and is the venue for the prestigious annual Queen Elisabeth Music Competition.

Almost at the end of the street and before you get to the main entrance of Bozar on the corner with Rue Ravenstein, look for a plaque on the building high above a narrow window. Placed by the Brontë Society in 1979, it reads:

> Near this site formerly stood the Pensionnat Heger where the writers Charlotte and Emily Brontë studied in 1842–43. This commemorative plaque was placed here by the Brontë Society with the kind permission of the Palais des Beaux-Arts/Paleis voor Schone Kunsten 28-9-79.

Rue Terarken and Hôtel Ravenstein

Turn left out of Rue Baron Horta into Rue Ravenstein. Just before you come to the Hôtel Ravenstein, a mansion on the left-hand side, Rue Ravenstein forms a bridge or viaduct over a small street at a lower level. Descend some steps to your left leading down to this little cul-de-sac and walk to the end of it. At the time of writing, next to a goods entrance to Bozar is a replica of the round blue literary plaques that mark places associated with writers all over Britain, surely the only one of its kind that can be seen in Belgium. Placed in 2004 by a Dutch Brontë enthusiast, it reads:

> This plaque commemorates the old Quartier Isabelle of which the Rue Terarken is a lucky survival. Charlotte and Emily Brontë would have passed this street when going to the Pensionnat Heger in the Rue d'Isabelle where they stayed in 1842–43. The memory of this area lives on in the vivid image Charlotte portrays in her novel *Villette*.

This cul-de-sac, Rue Terarken, is one of the few remaining sections of the low-lying cobbled streets of the Brontës' period. It was originally a much longer street that joined up with Rue d'Isabelle, and the Brontës might well have walked along it. To get to the Protestant chapel where they attended services on Sundays, for example, one convenient route would have been to go to the end of Rue d'Isabelle, into Rue Terarken and then along Rue Villa Hermosa.

Go back up the steps, which are the only ones still to be found on the site of one of a series of steps known as the 'Escaliers des Juifs' (in memory of the medieval Jewish quarter formerly located here) at the end of each of the narrow streets leading down to Rue Terarken from Montagne de la Cour.

Continue past the splendid Hôtel Ravenstein or Cleves-Ravenstein, a fifteenth-century mansion of the Burgundian period and according to some accounts the birthplace of Henry VIII's fourth wife Anne of Cleves. Only the part of the building nearest the steps, before you come to the entrance to the courtyard, dates from the fifteenth century; the part beyond that is a twentieth-century imitation.

Mont des Arts

Before bearing left up Montagne de la Cour towards Place Royale, pause at the top of Mont des Arts, whose stairways and gardens slope down from the art museums towards the Gare Centrale, for one of the best views over Brussels. You can see the spire of the Town Hall in Grand Place below. This will give you a good idea of the difference in levels between the Haute-Ville (Upper Town), developed in the eighteenth century, and the old Basse-Ville (Lower Town). Charlotte Brontë highlights the contrast between the old and new towns to great effect in *Villette*. Rue d'Isabelle was at an intermediate level on the hill linking the two.

Rue Villa Hermosa

Walk up Montagne de la Cour. On the left-hand side, just before you come to the Musical Instruments Museum, is Rue Villa Hermosa, which like Rue Terarken is one of the few fragments of the old quarter to survive the twentieth-century redevelopment and which is cut short by the Bozar building. It originally terminated in steps leading down to Rue Terarken, but these disappeared when Bozar was built. It is named after the Duke of Villahermosa, a seventeenth-century governor of the Spanish Netherlands. In the nineteenth century it was well known for the Prince of Wales tavern, which was visited by Dickens and Thackeray.

The Protestant Chapel, 'Chapelle Royale'

Before you get to Place Royale cross over to the right-hand side of Montagne de la Cour and make your way to Place du Musée, hidden away behind the art museums.

This beautiful courtyard is one of the surprises of Brussels. The neoclassical buildings lining it originally formed part of the palace built in the 1760s by the Archduke Charles of Lorraine, a governor of the Austrian Netherlands, whose statue stands at the side of the square.

In a concave crescent-shaped wing of the buildings you will see four doors. The one on the right is the entrance to the 'Chapelle Royale' where Charlotte and Emily went on Sundays, which has been used for Protestant services since Napoleon granted the Protestants freedom to worship in 1804. During the period of Dutch rule (1815–30) it was used by the Dutch royal family, and in the Brontës' time the Protestant King Leopold I was one of the worshippers. Services were taken by the King's chaplain, the Reverend Evan Jenkins, whose wife recommended the Pensionnat Heger to the Brontës and invited them to lunch every Sunday – an invitation she came to regret because of the sisters' taciturnity.

In Chapter 19 of *The Professor* Charlotte compares the dress sense of the English congregation unfavourably with that of the *bruxellois* on their way to mass.

> Gracious goodness! why don't they dress better? 'My
> eye is yet filled with visions of the high-flounced,
> slovenly and tumbled dresses in costly silk and satin,

of the large, unbecoming collars in expensive lace, of the ill-cut coats and strangely-fashioned pantaloons which every Sunday, at the English service, filled the chairs of the Chapel royal and after it, issuing forth into the square, came into disadvantageous contrast with freshly and trimly attired foreign figures, hastening to attend *salut* . . .

If you can time your walk to arrive when the chapel is open for a service, you might be able to have a peek inside. It is little changed since the Brontës' time. Its bright cream-and-gilt decoration, painted ceiling and cherubs must have been in striking contrast to the somewhat dark and austere interior of their father's church of St Michael and All Angels in Haworth.

In 1842 the triennial art exhibition or 'Salon' was held in the Musée des Beaux-Arts housed in Charles de Lorraine's palace. Two of the paintings Charlotte saw there, Edouard de Biefve's *Une Almée* – which she renames 'Cleopatra' – and Fanny Geefs' *The Life of a Woman*, inspired the scathing description of two pictures in a gallery visited by Lucy Snowe in Chapter 19 of *Villette*. Lucy describes the women depicted in the latter painting as 'brainless nonentities'. Fanny Geefs (née Corr) was a Brussels-born artist of Irish descent, whose husband Guillaume Geefs sculpted the Belliard statue.

Place Royale

Walk out of Place du Musée and turn right into Place Royale, one of the few places in Brussels that has changed little since the Brontës' time. It was built on the site of the splendid old Coudenberg palace on the top of the Coudenberg ('cold hill'). The old palace burned down in 1731, and in the 1770s Charles of Lorraine commissioned the French architects Nicolas Barré and Barnabé Guimard to create the present neoclassical square; Guimard was responsible for much of the new Royal Quarter built round the park, including the

Palais de la Nation (parliament building). The statue of Godfrey of Bouillon, who was one of the leaders of the first crusade in the eleventh century, was erected in 1848, after the Brontës' time.

Cross Rue de la Régence and you will come to the entrance to Rue de Namur. On Sundays the Brontës used to walk up this street, through the city gateway of the Porte de Namur and along Chaussée d'Ixelles, for the dreaded Sunday lunches at the home of the Jenkins family.

The neoclassical church with its pillared portico and cupola is Saint Jacques sur Coudenberg. The Hegers worshipped at this church, which was where the investiture of Leopold I, first King of the Belgians, took place on 21 July 1831.

On Lucy's arrival in Brussels on a cold wet night she gets lost looking for an inn to which she has been directed and describes a scene that may have been prompted by Charlotte's memory of St Jacques and Place Royale:

> On I went, hurrying fast through a magnificent street and square, with the grandest houses round, and amidst them the huge outline of more than one overbearing pile; which might be palace, or church – I could not tell. Just as I passed a portico, two moustachioed men came suddenly from behind the pillars; they were smoking cigars . . . They spoke with insolence, and, fast as I walked, they kept pace with me a long way. (*Villette*, Chapter 7)

Walk past the church to the BELvue museum, which tells the history of Belgium since the revolution. It was formerly the Hôtel Bellevue, where Charlotte's idol the Duke of Wellington stayed at the time of Waterloo. During the Belgian Revolution the building was used as a base by the insurgents in the battle with Dutch troops that raged for four days (23–26 September 1830) in the square and park and on the Belliard steps.

Through this museum you can access the archaeological site of the long-demolished Coudenberg Palace and walk on a part of the Rue d'Isabelle which has been excavated, the part which orig-inally led to the palace. It is an eerie experience to tread its cobbles underground. You are not following literally in the Brontës' foot-steps, however, since they could never have walked on this particular stretch of the street. It was buried at the time of the late-eighteenth-century redevelopment of Place Royale, when the height of the square was raised substantially.

The Park

Leave Place Royale by the Rue Royale side and enter the park from Place des Palais, in front of the Royal Palace.

The palace has had a chequered history. The building the Brontës knew was the result of a conversion of two town houses that was carried out in 1815–29. Since then the structure has under-gone numerous alterations.

The Park was redesigned by Barnabé Guimard and Joachim Zinner at the time of the redevelopment of the royal quarter in the 1770s. In its heyday it teemed with the fashionable *bruxellois* and visitors to the city staying in the nearby hotels. It was in the park that Wellington, asked on the eve of Waterloo whether he thought he would win the coming battle, pointed to a British soldier stroll-ing under the trees and replied that the outcome depended on whether 'he had enough of that article'.

Walk to the *kiosque à musique*, the bandstand, in Charlotte and Emily's day a brand-new construction designed by the up-and-coming architect Cluysenaar. They are likely to have attended concerts here during festivities such as the commemoration of the 1830 Revolution or the Feast of the Assumption. A concert at a *kiosque* is mentioned in Chapter 38 of *Villette*, in which Lucy leaves her bed to join the crowd in the park at a midnight fête.

Erected in 1841, the bandstand was first placed near the north gate of the park opposite the Belgian parliament building on the site occupied today by the Grand Bassin (large pond) before being moved to its present location in 1846.

Have a look at the Petit Bassin near by, an octagonal-shaped pool that may have been the one Charlotte had in mind when she describes how Lucy's longing to stand near the cool waters of a 'stone basin' in the park makes her leave her bed and head for it on a stifling midsummer night.

Exit the park opposite the Belliard statue, which was the starting point of our walk. Turn right and walk along Rue Royale past the Parc metro station and across Rue de la Loi on your right, where the parliament building stands. The next street off to the right is Rue de Louvain. The Brontës would have walked along it to the Porte de Louvain (on the site of Place Madou today) and thence along Chaussée de Louvain to the Protestant cemetery to visit the grave of their friend Martha Taylor, who died of cholera at her school in Koekelberg on the outskirts of the city. This is the route taken in *The Professor* by William Crimsworth on his way to the Protestant cemetery where he is reunited with Frances Henri. The cemetery, which stood roughly at the intersection of Chaussée de Louvain and Rue du Noyer, no longer exists, and the Chaussée, a country road in the Brontës' time, is now a busy shopping street.

Cross Rue Royale at this point and make your way down Treurenberg to the Cathedral.

The Cathedral

The Gothic Cathedral of Saint Gudule was the scene of Charlotte's confession to a Catholic priest on the evening of I September 1843, during a period of depression in the school summer holidays when she was left practically alone at the Pensionnat. She recounted this adventure in a letter to Emily the following day (see Chapter 17) and also used the episode in Chapter 15 of *Villette*.

Given Charlotte's virulent anti-Catholicism, her sudden impulse to confess was startling, to say the least. It appears to have been prompted by a combination of motives: general depression, loneliness and the need to talk to someone, boredom – the desire for a new sensation – and very possibly the mental torment caused by her growing infatuation with her tutor Constantin Heger.

The Collegiate Church of St Michael and St Gudule, patron saints of Brussels, was chiefly constructed between the thirteenth and fifteenth centuries, although the original Romanesque church dates back to the eleventh century and there was a chapel to St Michael on the site in the ninth. In Charlotte's time it was not yet officially a cathedral (although often referred to as such), since Brussels came under the diocese of Mechelen. It was not until 1962 that it was granted equal status with the Cathedral of Mechelen in the archdiocese of Mechelen-Brussels.

Tradition has it that the confession box Charlotte used was the second on the left-hand side.

Other Places with Brontë Connections

You could also take a look at the Théâtre Royal, the opera house, in Place de la Monnaie. Here Charlotte may have seen the famous French actress 'Rachel' (Eliza Rachel Félix), 'Vashti' in *Villette*, although the 'Vashti' section (Chapter 23) is at least partly based on a performance she saw some years later in London. The building Charlotte knew burned down in the 1850s, but was similar in style to the one there today. Unfortunately the square itself has changed rather more since her time. It was then one of the most elegant and fashionable after Place Royale, full of cafés where smart gentlemen smoked their cigars.

On 25 August 1830, at the height of disaffection with Dutch rule, the theatre was the setting for the outbreak of the Belgian Revolution when the opera *La Muette de Portici*, about a fisherman who led an uprising against Spanish rule in seventeenth-century Naples, moved members of the audience to pour out into the street and join workers rioting at a time of popular unrest after a bad harvest. The ensuing revolt against the Dutch ruler William I led to Belgian independence.

You could also go to see Place des Martyrs, which Charlotte mentions in Chapter 38 of *Villette* in some typically dismissive

Place de la Monnaie. On the left is the Théâtre Royal, where Charlotte may have seen the French actress Rachel, 'Vashti' in *Villette*, when she performed in Brussels in the summer of 1842.
From Alphonse Wauters, Les Délices de la Belgique, *Société des Beaux Arts, Brussels, 1844*

Place des Martyrs and the monument to the Belgian insurgents killed in the 1830 Revolution by F. Stroobant
Brussels City Archives

remarks on the Belgian Revolution. The monument over the crypt with the remains of the 445 insurgents killed in the revolt was erected in 1838. The statue representing the Motherland with the Belgian lion at her feet was created by Guillaume Geefs, who sculpted the statue of Belliard. The square was one of those redeveloped in the late eighteenth century, and the neoclassical (Louis XVI) buildings are typical of the city in the Brontës' time.

Further afield, you could visit the grave of Constantin Heger, his wife and one of their daughters, Marie, on the outskirts of the city in the attractive Watermael-Boitsfort municipal cemetery (Rue du Buis 57, 1170 Brussels) on the edge of the Fôret de Soignes. Heger died in 1896 at the age of eighty-six.

The Heger grave in the Watermael-Boitsfort cemetery

A VERY BRIEF HISTORY OF BELGIUM UP TO INDEPENDENCE

The Brontës arrived in Belgium not long after it became an independent state.

In the Middle Ages the region known as the Low Countries – modern-day Belgium, the Netherlands and Luxembourg – was a patchwork of small states including the Duchy of Brabant, whose capital Brussels became.

In the fifteenth century the region came under the more centralized rule of the Dukes of Burgundy and in the sixteenth under that of the Spanish Hapsburgs, notably the Emperor Charles V and his son Philip II. In 1585, after years of war against Spanish rule – in 1567 Philip II sent the Duke of Alba to Brussels to quell a Protestant rising – the northern part of the Low Countries became independent and Protestant (the modern-day Netherlands), while the Southern Netherlands continued under Spanish rule.

In the eighteenth century, after the War of the Spanish Succession, they were governed by the Austrian Hapsburgs and known as the Austrian Netherlands. In 1794 the French revolutionary armies incorporated them into France. After Napoleon's fall from power they were ruled from 1815 to 1830 by the Dutch King William I, whose authoritarian ways – for example, his attempt to impose the Dutch language on French-speaking functionaries – led to the 1830 Revolution and independence.

Belgium was recognized as an independent state at the London Conference of 1830, and a new constitution was enacted on 7 February 1831. Leopold of Saxe-Coburg was invited to become the first King of the Belgians and was crowned on 21 July 1831.

PLOT SUMMARIES OF CHARLOTTE'S BRUSSELS NOVELS VILLETTE AND THE PROFESSOR

Villette

Villette, the second and best of Charlotte Bronte's two 'Brussels novels', is set in a boarding-school that is in practically every detail the Pensionnat Heger. It has a prelude that takes place in England, but for many readers the real interest of the story begins once its heroine Lucy Snowe arrives in Brussels.

In the first three chapters we see her as a girl of thirteen or fourteen, staying with her godmother Mrs Bretton and the latter's sixteen-year-old son, Graham. At this stage we get little real impression of Lucy, who appears cold and impassive, and attention is focused on a child called Polly, a relative of the Brettons who is also staying with them while her father is abroad. The motherless little girl pines for him but in his absence transfers her devotion to the handsome Graham until her father takes her away again. Lucy, too, leaves, to return to a home with uncongenial relatives. She loses sight of the Brettons and Polly, and their relevance to the rest of the novel does not become clear to us until later on. We gather that Lucy is an orphan and unhappy, but we are given no details of her tribulations. We next see her, alone in the world having somehow lost all her relatives, earning a living as a companion to an invalid lady. When her employer dies she decides to seek her fortune as an English teacher on the continent. From now on her experiences

Lucy Snowe ringing the bell at the door of Mme Beck's Pensionnat.
The school imagined by the illustrator does not bear much
resemblance to Mme Heger's.
E.M. Wimperis, illustration for Villette, *Smith, Elder and Co., London, 1873*

coincide in many points with Charlotte's. Like her, she stays at an
old inn near St Paul's and is rowed out into the Thames to spend
a night on the steamer leaving for Boue-Marine ('Sea mud', that
is, Ostend) the next morning.

On the crossing she meets a frivolous English girl, Ginevra
Fanshawe, who is returning to school in Villette ('little town', that
is, Brussels), the capital of Labassecour ('the farmyard', that is,
Belgium). Ginevra suggests that Lucy seek employment as a
'nursery-governess' to the young children of the school's directress,
Mme Beck. On arrival at Villette that night she is given directions
to an inn by another traveller, a handsome young Englishman, but
gets lost and instead ends up in Rue Fossette (for which read 'Rue
d'Isabelle') in front of Mme Beck's Pensionnat de Demoiselles.
When Lucy enquires about employment, Mme Beck, with the
approval of M. Paul, a relative of hers who teaches at the school,
hires her to look after her children.

At first Lucy is confined to the nursery and to critically observ-ing the little world of Rue Fossette and Mme Beck's methods of governing by espionage. However, after standing in one day for the English master, she is promoted to the position of teacher. But life is still monotonous, and she longs for something to 'lead her upwards and outwards'. Unlike the flirtatious Ginevra, who is courted by a count called De Hamal and another suitor she calls Isidore, Lucy has no admirers.

At this point a handsome young English doctor known as 'Dr John' enters this little world when one of the children falls sick. Lucy recognizes him as the man who directed her on her first night.

By contrast with the tall fair-haired doctor, M. Paul, small, dark and irritable, initially seems unattractive. But from the start he is the only person in the school who represents passion, as he rages at his pupils' unresponsiveness to literature and tries to inject feeling into their performances in the school play. He coerces Lucy into standing in for one of the actors and locks her in the attic to learn her part, although by making sure she has a tasty supper he proves to be a benevolent tyrant. To her own surprise she enjoys her taste of acting, a rare experience of being more than a passive onlooker of life. Ginevra's two suitors are present at the ensuing dance, and Lucy learns that 'Isidore' is none other than Dr John, who is besotted with Ginevra.

M. Paul recognizes in Lucy someone as passionate and fiery as himself, someone who is not the shrinking violet she appears. He is the only person to see her true nature; to everyone else, including Dr John, she seems 'a colourless shadow'. She, in her turn, gradually comes to understand the true nature of M. Paul.

In one of the most autobiographical episodes of the novel Lucy describes her depression alone in the Pensionnat in the summer holidays. Her despair drives her to the confessional of a Catholic church. When she faints in the street on leaving the church she is rescued by Dr John, who takes her to La Terrasse, the home he shares with his mother on the outskirts of Brussels. By one of the novel's more improbable coincidences, the two turn out to be Mrs Bretton and her son Graham. He has hitherto failed to recognize her as the Lucy he used to know. Lucy, on the other hand, now reveals to the reader for the first time that she recognized him some time ago but enjoyed keeping her identity secret from him.

During her stay at La Terrasse she is increasingly attracted to Graham, and they become friends although he continues to sing Ginevra's praises. However, his eyes are at last opened to Ginevra's real nature at a concert where he sees her making fun of his mother and flirting with De Hamal.

The Brettons show Lucy around the city's attractions. M. Paul has a habit of popping up at the galleries and concert halls she visits with her new friends and she realizes that his rudeness whenever he sees her with Graham is caused by jealousy.

Back at the Pensionnat, only Graham's letters relieve the monotony of her life. She longs for his love although her rational self knows that he is not for her and M. Paul warns her that this love is poisoning her life.

While reading a letter from Graham in the attic, where she has retreated for privacy, she is terrified by the sight of a nun, a phantom she is to see on several occasions. Is it a hallucination, or the ghost of a nun who was buried alive in the garden for some sin in the days when a convent stood on the site?

A fire at a theatre she is attending with the Brettons introduces us to some new arrivals in Villette who turn out to be old acquaintances of Lucy's. A beautiful girl called Paulina whom Graham rescues in the stampede is none other than the little Polly who adored him when he was a teenager. Her father has inherited the title of Count De Bassompierre and they are living at the Hôtel Crécy.

Paulina and Graham fall in love and it is to Paulina that he sends the love letter Lucy never had from him and always longed for. Resignedly, she buries her own letters from him in the garden, where she again sees the mysterious nun. She renounces any hope of love; her only aspiration now is to start her own school.

Her stormy relationship with M. Paul, who sees her intellectual potential and has started to tutor her, now develops into friendship and he calls her his 'little sister'. Mme Beck has her eye on him as a possible match for herself and tries to drive the two apart by having Lucy informed that he is faithful to the memory of his long-dead fiancée, who took the veil when forbidden to marry him. (Is *she* the nun of the ghostly visitations?) However, knowledge of his past only increases Lucy's admiration of him when she learns that he lives in poverty in order to support the dead woman's grandmother – the repulsive Mme Walravens – and various hangers-on including his spiritual adviser Père Silas, the old priest who heard Lucy's confession.

Despite Père Silas' warnings to M. Paul to steer clear of Lucy as a dangerous heretic, and M. Paul's unsuccessful attempts to convert her to Catholicism, the friendship between the two prospers. But just as it is deepening into something more it is suddenly announced that M. Paul is leaving for three years to attend to business in the West Indies, apparently with no thought of Lucy. Mme Beck gives her an opiate to make her sleep after she has had an emotional outburst. Yet she is unable to sleep and, under the influence of the drug, as if in a dream, she leaves her bed and finds herself at midnight among a crowd of revellers in the park, illuminated for a *fête*. Here she sees M. Paul and the whole of the 'secret junta' which is plotting to separate her from him – Mme Beck, Père Silas and Mme Walravens. She learns that it is they who are sending him to the West Indies to attend to Mme Walravens' business interests there. Observing M. Paul with the wealthy young Justine Marie, the niece of his dead fiancée, Lucy concludes that he is to marry her as a reward for his services.

On returning to the dormitory she sees what appears to be the nun lying on her bed. It is in fact a nun's habit put there as a joke by Ginevra, who has eloped that night with De Hamal. It turns out that the nun's appearances have a disappointingly prosaic explanation: De Hamal used to climb into the Pensionnat and disguise himself in the habit on clandestine visits to Ginevra.

"QUE ME VOULEZ-VOUS?" SAID SHE
HOARSELY

Lucy goes to Mme Walravens' house.
Edmund Dulac, illustration for Villette, Dent, London, 1922

M. Paul is due to sail shortly. Just as Lucy has given up any hope of seeing him before he leaves, he reappears. Defying a final attempt by Mme Beck to come between them, he takes her to see a little house in the faubourgs which – the explanation of his three-week silence – he has rented and been busy furnishing for her. Here she is to live and open a school while she waits for his return from his travels. She is assured of his love and learns that she has nothing to fear from Justine Marie, who is his goddaughter, not his fiancée.

"I CALL HERE," SAID HE

M. Paul takes Lucy to the little house he has rented for her.
Edmund Dulac, illustration for Villette, *Dent, London, 1922*

After a few blissful hours together in Lucy's little house he departs for the West Indies. The next three years spent making a success of her school and waiting for his return are the happiest of her life because of the delight of receiving his letters.

At the time of M. Paul's return voyage, raging storms 'strew the Atlantic with wrecks'. Lucy refrains from stating in so many words that he is one of the many lost at sea, preferring to leave those readers who so wish to 'picture union and a happy succeeding life'.

But, in the light of her statement that the three years of their correspondence were the happiest of her life, this outcome seems unlikely. Charlotte Brontë rejects a conventional happy ending in favour of one that is, at best, ambiguous.

Autobiographical elements in *Villette*

The most obvious autobiographical references in *Villette* are the Brussels setting, life at the Pensionnat and Charlotte's relationship with M. Heger. But the novel was written almost ten years after her stay in Brussels and more recent circumstances in her life also found their way into it. She wrote it soon after the death of Branwell, Emily and Anne. She was now living alone with her father, his sole surviving child, hearing, as she wrote, the wind keening around a much more silent Parsonage. Lucy, too, is a lonely survivor, of unspecified disasters that lead to the loss of all her family connections. Charlotte's recent bereavements and consequent desolation darkened the atmosphere of her last novel.

Her hopes and disappointments in love found their way into its pages, too. Although it is ultimately a story of wish-fulfilment, of the relationship she would have liked with Heger, she also explored in it another real-life relationship – with her publisher George Smith, the model for Graham Bretton. She even took Smith's mother, who lived with him and often invited Charlotte to stay with them in London, as the model for Mrs Bretton. When they first met at the time of the publication of *Jane Eyre* Charlotte was thirty-two and the charming and good-looking Smith was twenty-seven. The two became friends, mainly by correspondence. Charlotte was attracted to him and at one stage seems, against her better judgement, to have hoped for more than just friendship. She looked forward eagerly to his letters, although perhaps not as desperately as she had once longed for Heger's.

Lucy's renunciation of any hope of Graham's love and her decision to bury his letters doubtless echo Charlotte's own despondency about the likelihood of a future with Smith. These fears were confirmed when she learned soon after the publication of *Villette* of his engagement to someone younger, prettier and richer than herself.

In the concluding part of the novel she revisited her old love for Heger. As she wrote the last chapters she can have had little or no hope of ever experiencing the fulfilment Lucy finds, albeit briefly, with her Belgian 'professor'. For most of the novel she explores the lot of a woman facing life alone. And on the final page we feel pretty certain that Lucy is left facing the future, once again, alone. She won her professor's love but she is not allowed to live with him happily ever after.

Since her youth Charlotte had been struggling bravely to come to terms with life as a single woman. But at the age of thirty-seven, with all her siblings dead and her father old and frail, her solitude became too great to bear. Soon after Smith married, she herself decided to accept an offer of marriage from Arthur Bell Nicholls. He had none of the intellectual brilliance or charisma of a Constantin Heger or a George Smith. She had known him as her father's curate for years but never thought of him as a possible partner until he told her that he had loved her all those years. She died after only nine months of what turned out to be a happy union. Her final destiny was thus very different from that of Lucy, who lives into old age as a single professional woman. But, like Lucy's, Charlotte's course through life was a troubled one, a struggle rather than the charmed existence of a Ginevra or a Paulina.

The Professor

The Professor, written soon after Charlotte left Brussels but not published till after her death, is a much less polished work than *Villette* but interesting as a first novel drawing on her Brussels years, a trial run for the later book. It is also interesting as a record of her impressions of Brussels while they were still fresh and without the disguise of fictitious names employed in *Villette*.

Like the later novel it has a prelude set in England, in a northern industrial town where the narrator, William Crimsworth, is employed – rather improbably, as a translator – by his tyrannical elder brother, a mill-owner. His only friend is the outspoken Hunsden, also a manufacturer, who shares his interest in foreign languages and literature. When Crimsworth gives up his uncongenial employment Hunsden suggests that he seek a post in Brussels.

Once there Crimsworth soon finds work as an English master at a school run by a M. Pelet. Just as in real life the Athenée Royal – the boys' school where M. Heger taught – was next door to the Pensionnat Heger, so Pelet's school (inspired by a boarding-house run by a M. Lebel near the Athénée Royal in Brussels) is next to the girls' boarding-school run by the efficient Zoraïde Reuter. The name is somewhat reminiscent of Zoë Heger, and when Zoraïde hires Crimsworth to give classes at her school we are not surprised to find numerous parallels between Mme Heger's school and Mlle Reuter's or between Charlotte Brontë's impressions of her pupils and William Crimsworth's of his.

Crimsworth admires Zoraïde and is initially attracted by her. She encourages his attentions, but he discovers that she and Pelet are engaged to be married and that she is playing a double game. Realizing that the qualities he admired in her are a sham, he transfers his attentions to the shy Frances Evans Henri, a young Anglo-Swiss girl who teaches lace-mending at the school and attends his English classes. Frances writes compositions in English for Crimsworth, just as Charlotte herself had written French essays for Heger. Again, we are not surprised when the teacher–pupil relationship quickly develops into love.

Jealously observing this, Zoraïde banishes Frances from her school. Not knowing where she lives, Crimsworth combs the streets of Brussels in search of her and eventually finds her visiting her aunt's grave in the Protestant cemetery.

After this reunion everything goes smoothly for the pair. They declare their love for each other, marry, start their own school, have a son and after ten years' hard work are wealthy enough

BUT SHE RAISED HERSELF ON HER TIPTOES,
AND PLUCKING A BRANCH OF LILAC,
OFFERED IT TO ME WITH GRACE

Crimsworth with Mlle Reuter in the garden of her Pensionnat
Edmund Dulac, illustration for The Professor, *Dent, London, 1922*

to retire to England where they settle near Crimsworth's old friend Hunsden.

In this first novel Charlotte Brontë drew on her feelings for Heger to explore a romantic teacher–pupil relationship from the perspective of the teacher, the man. This is not the only element of her Brussels experience that is inverted in the novel. Heger tutored Charlotte in French; Crimsworth tutors Frances in English. Frances gets a job teaching French at an English school; Charlotte was employed as an English teacher at a French-speaking school. But in some essential ways Frances is an idealized version of Charlotte. Like her, she appears diffident but is in fact fully aware of her capacities and has considerable *amour-propre* and ambition. She is not satisfied until she is running her own school and is professionally and financially on a par with her husband.

NOTES

Abbreviations: Smith: Smith, Margaret (ed.), *The Letters of Charlotte Brontë.* Volume I, 1829–1847, Clarendon Press, Oxford, 1995

PL: Ruijssenaars, Eric, *Charlotte Brontë's Promised Land: The Pensionnat Heger and Other Brontë Places in Brussels,* Brontë Society, Haworth, Yorkshire, 2000

Chapter 2: What Brought the Brontës to Brussels?

1 Letter to Elizabeth Branwell, 29 September 1841; Smith, pp. 268–9.
2 Letter to Ellen Nussey, 9 December 1841; Smith, p. 274.
3 Letter to Ellen Nussey, 7 August 1841; Smith, p. 266.

Chapter 4: Charlotte and Emily at the Pensionnat

1 Letter to Ellen Nussey, May 1842; Smith, p. 284.
2 Charlotte Brontë, 'Prefatory Note to "Selections from Poems by Ellis Bell"', in Margaret Smith (ed.), *The Letters of Charlotte Brontë,* Volume II, p. 753.

Chapter 5: Monsieur Heger

1 Letter to Branwell Brontë, 1 May 1843; Smith, p. 317.
2 Letter to Ellen Nussey, May 1842; Smith, p. 284.
3 Comment written by Heger on Charlotte's essay *The Nest*; Sue Lonoff (ed.), *The Belgian Essays: A Critical Edition,* Yale University Press, New Haven, Conn., 1996, p. 42.
4 Lonoff, pp. 244–6.
5 Lonoff, p. 248.

6 Elizabeth Gaskell, *The Life of Charlotte Brontë*, London, 1857, Chapter 11.

7 Frederika MacDonald, *The Secret of Charlotte Brontë*, London, 1914, Part II, Chapter 2.

Chapter 8: Extract from Villette (1)

1 Here! This is for you.

2 Do you intend to insult me?

3 Come, come.

4 Isn't that so?

5 You're only young once.

6 I understand, I understand: one knows the definition of 'friend'. Good Day, Miss!

7 I can see that you make fun of me and my belongings.

Chapter 9: A Look Back at the History of the Isabelle Quarter

1 Gerald Cumberland, 'Charlotte Brontë's Street in Brussels Today', *Cornhill Magazine*, Vol. 30, May 1911; Reprinted in *PL*, pp. 84–6.

Chapter 13: The Brontës' Friends in Brussels

1 *Shirley*, Chapter 9.

2 Letter from Mary and Martha Taylor and Charlotte Brontë to Ellen Nussey, March–April 1842; Smith, pp. 280–82.

Chapter 14: Brussels in the Brontës' Time

1 William Makepeace Thackeray, 'Little Travels and Roadside Sketches', *Fraser's Magazine*, May 1844.

2 Composition dated 5 June 1843; Smith, p. 323.

Chapter 16: Charlotte's Second Year in Brussels

1 Letter to Ellen Nussey, 10 November 1842; Smith, p. 302.

Chapter 17: The Confession at St Gudule's

1 Letter to Ellen Nussey, July 1842; Smith, pp. 289–90.

2 I could not enjoy the privilege of confession.

3 Letter to Emily Brontë, 2 September 1843. Smith, pp. 329–30.

Chapter 18: Leaving Brussels

1 Letter to Victoire Dubois, 18 May 1844; Smith, p. 346.

Chapter 19: After Brussels: Writing to M. Heger

1 Letter to M. Heger, 8 January 1845; Smith, p. 379.
2 Letter to M. Heger, 18 November 1845; Smith, p. 436.

Chapter 21: After Brussels: Fame

1 M.H. Spielmann, *The Inner History of the Brontë–Heger Letters*, Chapman and Hall, London, 1919.
2 See Brian Bracken, 'Marion Spielmann's Brontë–Heger Letters History: Fact or Fiction?', *Brontë Studies*, Vol. 38, No. 1, January 2013.

Chapter 22: The Pensionnat Becomes a Place of Pilgrimage

1 Adeline Trafton, 'A Visit to Charlotte Brontë's School at Brussels', *Scribner's Monthly*, Vol. 3, No. 2, December 1871; reprinted in *PL*, pp. 58–60.
2 Gerald Cumberland, *op.cit.*
3 *The Professor*, Chapter 7.
4 M.H. Spielmann, 'Charlotte Brontë in Brussels: A Nursery of Genius – New Light on the Novels', *Times Literary Supplement*, 1916; reprinted in *PL*, pp. 93–101.

SELECT READING LIST

There are a great number of books on Charlotte and Emily Brontë. This very short list of suggested reading includes the most complete biography of the whole family (Juliet Barker's The Brontës*). It also includes Elizabeth Gaskell's classic biography of Charlotte Brontë, a couple of more recent ones and some works that shed light on the sisters' stay in Brussels.*

Barker, Juliet, *The Brontës*, Abacus, London, 2010 (revised edition)

Blyth, Derek, *Brussels for Pleasure: Thirteen Walks Through the Historic City* (see Walk 6, 'Charlotte Brontë and the Royal Quarter'), Pallas Athene, London, 2004

Chadwick, Ellis H., *In the Footsteps of the Brontës*, Pitman and Sons, London, 1914

Gaskell, Elizabeth, *The Life of Charlotte Brontë*, Smith, Elder and Co., London, 1857

Gérin, Winifred, *Charlotte Brontë*, Clarendon Press, Oxford, 1971

Gérin, Winifred, *Charlotte Brontë: The Evolution of Genius*, Clarendon Press, Oxford, 1967

Gordon, Lyndall, *Charlotte Brontë: A Passionate Life*, Chatto and Windus, London, 1994

Lonoff, Sue (ed.), *The Belgian Essays: A Critical Edition*, Yale University Press, New Haven, Conn., 1996

MacDonald, Frederika, *The Secret of Charlotte Brontë*, T.C. and E.C. Jack, London, 1914 (also available online at www.gutenberg.org)

Ruijssenaars, Eric, *Charlotte Brontë's Promised Land: The Pensionnat Heger and Other Brontë Places in Brussels*, Brontë Society, Haworth, Yorkshire, 2000. Includes some interesting articles by literary pilgrims about their visits to the Pensionnat and their reflections on the sisters' time there, for example, Adeline Trafton's 'A Visit to Charlotte Brontë's School at Brussels' (1871) and Marion Spielmann's 'Charlotte Brontë in Brussels: A Nursery of Genius' (1916).

Ruijssenaars E. *The Pensionnat Revisited: More Light Shed on the Brussels of the Brontës*, Dutch Archives, Leiden, 2003

Spielmann, M.H., *The Inner History of the Brontë–Heger Letters*, Chapman and Hall, London, 1919

Smith, Margaret, ed., *The Letters of Charlotte Brontë*, Volume I, 1829–1847, Clarendon Press, Oxford, 1995

INDEX